Gemini

you
can
never
have
enough

Zucchini

you
can
never
have
enough

by
John Butler

Introduction by
Lois Hole

HOLE'S

The University
of Alberta Press

Published by
  The University of Alberta Press
  Ring House 2
  Edmonton, Alberta T6G 2E1
and
  HOLE'S
  101 Bellerose Drive
  St. Albert, Alberta T8N 8N8

Printed in Canada   5   4   3   2   1
First Printing May 2001

National Library of Canada Cataloguing in Publication Data
Butler, John, 1947–
  Zucchini

  Copublished by: Hole's Greenhouses and Gardens.
  ISBN 0-88864-379-9

  1. Cookery (Zucchini) 2. Zucchini. I. Hole's Greenhouses &
Gardens. II. Title.
TX803.Z82B87 2001   641.6'562   C2001-910027-2

Printed and bound in Canada by Quality Color Press, Edmonton, Alberta.
Prepress by Elite Lithographers Co. Ltd.

The University of Alberta Press acknowledges the financial support of the Govern-
ment of Canada through the Book Publishing Industry Development Program for
its publishing activities. The Press also gratefully acknowledges the support received
for its program from the Canada Council for the Arts.

Zucchini: You Can Never Have Enough is a publication for the book trade.

Preface: Bountiful Gardens

Anyone who gardens knows that much of the enjoyment comes from the harvest, whether it's the vibrant beauty of bedding plants or the snap of a garden-fresh carrot.

The Bountiful Gardens series is designed to help you get more from the food plants you grow in your garden. Through these books, we hope you will bring the joys of the garden to your kitchen and table. We also hope you'll make healthy eating a regular habit throughout the year.

Part of the pleasure in gardening is sharing what you grow, and cooking is a perfect way to spread your joy. We hope that in making these recipes, you will be creating memories and traditions for years to come.

Contents

Acknowledgements
11

Introduction by Lois Hole
13

Cooking with Zucchini by John Butler
19

**Approximate Weight-Volume Equivalents
Of Common Dry Ingredients**
32

Imperial to Metric Conversion
33

SOUPS AND SALADS • 35
Start with the Best Varieties
36

APPETIZERS AND SIDE DISHES • 49
Growing Zucchini
50

ENTRÉES • 79
Zucchini Care and Nurture
80

**SWEET TREATS
AND BAKED GOODS • 109**
Harvest Time
110

DIPS AND SPREADS • 133
Zucchini: The Genus
134

Contents

SOUPS AND SALADS

Zucchini-Leek Soup 37

Zucchini Minestrina 38

Zucchini-Coconut-
Curry Soup 39

Zucchini Blender Gazpacho ... 40

Zucchini and Onion Salad 41

Grilled Zucchini Salad 42

Grated Zucchini Salad 43

Cool Corn Salad 44

Zucchini and Jicama Salad 45

Southwestern Salad 46

Garden Vegetable Salad 47

Zucchini and Spinach,
Italian Style 48

APPETIZERS AND SIDE DISHES

Zucchini Bites 51

Zucchini Toasts 52

Zucchini-Stuffed Mushrooms 53

Deep-Fried Zucchini 54

Zucchini-Wrapped Scallops 55

Tempura Zucchini Blossoms .. 56

Stuffed Zucchini Blossoms 57

Shrimp Wraps 58

Spring Rolls 59

Festive Spring Rolls 60

Zucchini Pastries 61

Steamed Zucchini Rings 62

Steamed Baby Zucchini 63

Oven-Baked Zucchini 64

Stuffed Zucchini Boats 65

Sweet and Sour Zucchini 66

Marinated Vegetable
Noodles 67

Marinated Zucchini 68

Baby Zucchini with
Peas and Corn 69

Sautéed Onions
with Zucchini 70

Stuffed Zucchini 71

Zucchini Stuffed
with Pine Nuts 72

Barley Risotto
with Zucchini 73

Polenta with Zucchini 74

Zucchini Fried Rice 75

Hash Browns
Southwestern Style 76

Zucchini Skillet Pancakes 77

Quick Zucchini Cakes 78

ENTRÉES

Salmon with Zucchini 81

Sea Bass with Lemongrass
and Zucchini 82

Zucchini-Rolled Sole 83

Crab Cakes 84

Baked Salmon
with Zucchini 85

Baked Meatloaf 86

Zucchini Frittata 87

Zucchini Soufflés 88

Ratatouille 89

Zucchini Curry
with Beans and Corn 90

Contents

Sautéed Zucchini with Herb
and Tomato Salsa 91

Vegetable Stew 92

Baby Zucchini Curry 93

Zucchini-Potato Patties 94

Baby Zucchini
with Tricolour Pasta 95

Bacon-Macaroni Bake 96

Layered Casserole 97

Zucchini Tuscana 98

Garden Casserole with
Herb Biscuit Topping 99

Rustic Pie 100

Zucchini Pie 101

Zucchini Phyllo Roll 102

Zucchini Wraps 103

World's Best Pizza Dough 104

Fresh Zucchini Pizza 106

Zucchini Calzone 107

Mini Zucchini Pizza 108

SWEET TREATS
AND BAKED GOODS

Baked Apples
with Dried Fruit 111

Zucchini-Lime Crisp 112

Zucchini Squares 113

Chocolate-Almond-
Zucchini Cake 114

Zucchini-Pear Cobbler 115

Chocolate-Zucchini
Brownies 116

Zucchini Cookies 116

Zucchini-Oatmeal Cookies 117

Homestyle Cookies 118

Zucchini-Cheese Muffins 119

Applesauce-Zucchini
Muffins 120

Blueberry-Zucchini Muffins 121

Spicy Zucchini Cupcakes 122

Chocolate Pecan-
Zucchini Loaf 123

Zucchini-Cranberry-
Pineapple Loaf 124

Chocolate and
Nut Zucchini Loaf 125

Low-Fat Zucchini Loaf 126

Zucchini-Ginger Loaf 127

Zucchini-Coconut
Quick Bread 128

Zucchini-Apple Pie 129

Lemon Custard Pie 130

Cheese and Zucchini
Powder Biscuits 131

Zucchini-Cornmeal Scones 132

DIPS AND SPREADS

Zucchini-Pineapple Salsa 135

Red Onion and
Zucchini Relish 136

Zucchini Chutney 137

Minted Chutney 138

Quick Zucchini Dip 139

Fresh Vegetable Dip 140

Zucchini Pickles 141

Quick Zucchini-Ginger Jam 142

Zucchini Paté 143

Acknowledgements

There have been chefs who have had an indelible influence on my understanding of all things culinary. Andre Louis Meuniere was my Chef de Cuisine during my apprenticeship in London. He developed in me an appreciation for the organization of a kitchen brigade, teamwork, and above all, his ultimate compassion and protection of his kitchen staff. Julia Child, who, for as long as I can remember, has never wavered from her belief that the foundation of classical cuisine is centred on the principles, philosophy, and language of French cooking. All students of the art owe her a debt of gratitude for her groundbreaking work on television and her excellent volumes of culinary literature. Alice Waters, who had the vision and courage to create an environment for the earth-to-table concept of using only foods that came from farmers who are sympathetic with the land and the purity of the food they produce. The Roux Brothers, who developed a style of cuisine that inspired me to look at new ways of food preparation using classical methods and then presenting food in a style that led to the beginning of my attraction to food as visual art. Charlie Trotter, who is an example of true genius. His imagination, knowledge, and freedom of expression with food come from an incredible understanding of the medium he has chosen as his creative palette. His freedom and comfort level working with food is extraordinary. A humanitarian, renaissance man and artist. Ferran Adria, who takes food into another realm. This Catalan chef is the conductor and orchestrator of interpretation who uses food in ways that challenge our ordinary perceptions. The Salvador Dali of culinary expressionism. We should watch and listen.

There are many names I could add to this list. I respect these people most for their courage and dedication, and for giving their time and energy to add to the quality of life for those less fortunate.

I must thank those dedicated to the artistic process who shared the vision for the creation of this book. Without their support, encouragement, and dedication, it would not have been possible. The creative teams at the University of Alberta Press and Hole's took a curious collection of recipes and carefully constructed them into the piece of magic you hold in your hand. My special thanks to Bruce Keith, Greg Brown, Earl Woods, and Lois Hole at Hole's. At the University of Alberta Press, Leslie Vermeer asked the right questions, edited, and turned my collected work into a well-crafted book.

My love and very special thanks to Shirlee, Elythe, and Brooke, who endured the perils of recipe testing and tasting. I would not have been able to do this without you.

My thanks to Anne Assaly, Lynn Berg, David Fitzpatrck, Deb Meany, and Liz Pegoraro for their assistance.

—John Butler

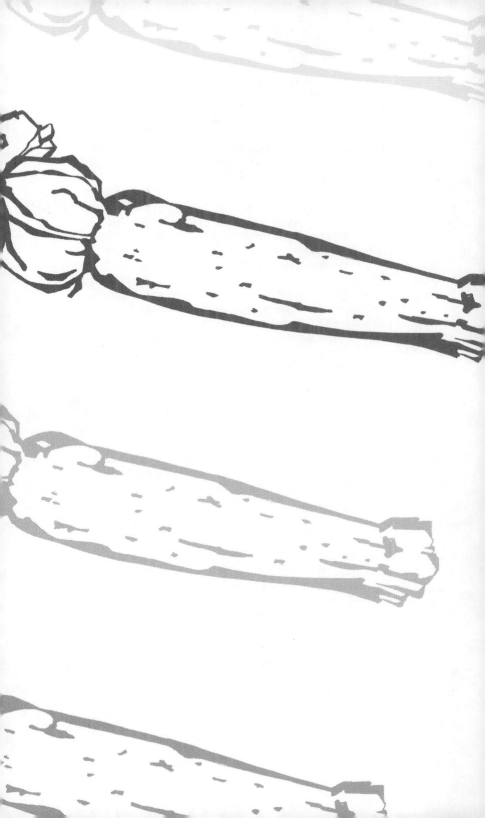

Introduction

by Lois E. Hole

You're probably not going to believe it, but I'm going to say it anyway: you can never have enough zucchini.

Maybe you'd call that statement outrageous, since almost everyone is aware of zucchini's notorious reputation for producing more fruit than anyone could ever possibly use. My friend Roger Swain loved to tell the story of a little town in Massachusetts where no one dared to leave their car doors unlocked or their windows rolled down in August. The danger wasn't car thieves; it was overburdened gardeners. Leave your car unlocked and untended for even a few minutes, he joked, and you'd return to find it stuffed with zucchini.

I remember a time, though, when no one in my neck of the woods had even heard of zucchini, much less had so much they needed to give it away. During the 1960s, my husband Ted and I ran a market gardening operation on our farm, helped by our two young sons, Bill and Jim. We had a pretty good selection of fresh produce, I thought, but when some recent immigrants from Italy asked for zucchini, I had no idea what they were talking about. Long, thick, and green? Cucumber, maybe? But no, that's not what they wanted. And soon some new Canadians from Lebanon and India began asking for the very same vegetable. There was obviously a market for this "exotic" plant, so I made sure that we grew some the next season.

I found out, though, that it wasn't simply a matter of planting a couple of rows and waiting for the harvest. Different people liked different kinds of zucchini. Immigrants from one part of Italy preferred their zucchini small, while other Italians loved the larger, more mature fruits. And picking zucchini while they were small encouraged the plant to produce even more fruit! We planted about a half acre every year; enough at the time to provide for the entire city of Edmonton, Bill liked to joke. He wasn't far from wrong.

Since zucchini matures so quickly, I often had to sow seed twice just to provide enough of the smaller fruits for the market. Zucchini grows so fast that it often got away from me. I usually had plenty of the big fruits, but few of the smaller, more delicate ones. So it wasn't long before (does this sound familiar?) we were giving away zucchini—at least the big ones! We sold produce out of our old red barn, and tucked away in one corner were our zucchini bins. "Free—take as many as you need!" proclaimed a hand-lettered sign. We had quite a few takers, but somehow those bins never were quite empty.

However, the vegetable's popularity did grow, inexorably, like the very fruit itself. It was an increasing number of recipes that drove demand for zucchini—recipes from the cultures of those immigrants who had first asked for the vegetable. The first thing I did with zucchini was to cut them in half, cover them with tomato sauce, and grate cheese over them; then, into the oven they went, just long enough to melt the cheese. It was a delicious treat, and one that we still enjoy today. My daughter-in-law Valerie also makes a delicious baked zucchini. It's one of her family's favourite dishes during the summer, when zucchini and tomatoes are plentiful.

Valerie's recipe

Valerie sometimes mixes different colours of cherry tomatoes for a combination of flavours and decorative effect. Try this recipe— it's easy and delicious!

Choose small to medium zucchini. Wash, remove the ends, and slice lengthwise in $\frac{1}{2}$-inch (1-cm) slices. Lay the slices on a lightly oiled cookie sheet. Beat an egg. Brush the egg over the upper surface of the zucchini slices. Grate cheddar cheese. (I prefer old cheddar because the flavour is stronger, but any cheddar or your favourite brick cheese will do.) Spread the grated cheese over the top of each zucchini slice. (Sometimes I also sprinkle fresh grated Parmesan on top of the grated cheddar for variety.) Slice some cherry tomatoes and lay them in a single layer on top of the cheese. Grate a little fresh pepper over the top. Bake in a 375°F (180°C) oven for 20 to 30 minutes, until the cheese is brown and bubbly. Serve immediately.

However, it was the more unusual recipes that made people pay serious attention to zucchini. Chocolate zucchini cake was probably the most popular offering, although fried zucchini, zucchini pizza, and zucchini sushi didn't lag far behind. One of my favourite zucchini recipes comes from the Best of Bridge cookbook. Here it is, because I think it's just wonderful!

Chocolate Zucchini Cake

Cream butter, oil, sugar, eggs, vanilla, and buttermilk. Sift dry ingredients and add to creamed mixture. Mix in zucchini and chocolate chips. Bake in a greased and floured bundt pan or a 9x13-inch (4-L) greased pan at 325°F (160°C) for 45 minutes. Delicious!

$\frac{1}{4}$ cup	butter	50 mL
$\frac{1}{2}$ cup	vegetable oil	125 mL
$1\frac{3}{4}$ cups	sugar	425 mL
2	eggs	2
1 tsp.	vanilla	5 mL
$\frac{1}{2}$ cup	buttermilk **or** sour milk	125 mL
$2\frac{1}{2}$ cups	flour	625 mL
4 tbsp.	cocoa	60 mL
$\frac{1}{2}$ tsp.	baking powder	2 mL
1 tsp.	baking soda	5 mL
$\frac{1}{2}$ tsp.	cinnamon	2 mL
$\frac{1}{2}$ tsp.	cloves	2 mL
2 cups	grated zucchini	500 mL
$\frac{1}{4}$ cup	chocolate chips	50 mL

In the 21st century, zucchini has found widespread popularity, thanks to both its remarkable versatility and several recent developments. Most importantly, new varieties of zucchini have been developed to improve its flavour and growth habit. Did you know that you can grow a yellow variety, or a more compact zucchini plant that's great for small gardens? Several of the best varieties are described in this book.

Another key to zucchini's acceptance among gardeners is the fact that it can be grown in almost any garden across Canada, given proper care. Basic horticultural information is included to help you get the most from this terrific plant. And you'll learn how to harvest zucchini at their prime, for the best possible flavour.

The key, however, to zucchini's new trendy status is our increasing willingness to experiment with it. Back when I was first introduced to this vegetable, I didn't use it for much. Little did I know that I had only scratched the surface of zucchini's potential. John Butler showed me what I was missing.

John provided many of the recipes for my book *Herbs & Edible Flowers*, and it was while we were working on that book that I learned what a warm and wonderful man he is. John brought many of his creations over to the house for me to try, spoiling me completely with his scrambled eggs with hops, candied pansies, pumpkin sunflower bread, and my favourite, lavender shortbread cookies. Lavender is my favourite herb, and my Auntie Anne always used to treat us with her shortbread cookies, but I'd never considered that the two could be combined. That's what I love about John: he's always coming up with fantastic new ways to enjoy old favourites.

John brought some of his new zucchini creations over to the publishing office during the making of this book, and everyone raved about the phyllo pastry with zucchini and the spicy zucchini-potato pancakes. Never in a million years would I have thought to use zucchini like this, but if there's one thing I've learned from John, it's that you shouldn't be afraid to experiment in the kitchen.

One of Canada's few Master Chefs, a Gold Medal winner, and the first Canadian recipient of the prestigious Julia Child Scholarship from the International Association of Culinary Professionals, John has the expertise and passion to take full advantage of zucchini's versatility. He's provided more than 100 scrumptious recipes, from breakfast to dessert and everything in between, and he's even included nutritional data for each recipe. John's introduction also provides presentation ideas, insight into his philosophy of cooking, his favourite methods, and much more. You'll never wonder what to do with zucchini again.

Too much zucchini? Nonsense! Once you've read this book, I'm sure you'll agree that you can never have enough!

Hey, Walter! You think six rows
of zucchini will be enough?

Grow your own zucchini!

• *Even if you're a rookie gardener, you can grow zucchini successfully in your garden. It's reliable, grows quickly and easily, and is almost completely disease and pest free.*

• *Add lots of compost to the part of the garden where you will plant the zucchini. The organic matter helps retain moisture and makes the soil soft and pliable, so the zucchini plants root well.*

• *Here's a simple method for raising a bumper crop of zucchini. Plant a row of 12 to 15 individual seeds spaced approximately 15 cm apart. As the seedlings emerge and become established, thin the plants to 30 cm. Thin them again as the plants get bigger (to about 60 cm, then 90 cm), leaving only 3 or 4 strong plants. Remember, zucchini is a squash, and most varieties need lots of room to grow. If your space is limited, try a compact variety like 'Spacemiser.'*

• *Many gardeners prefer to seed zucchini directly into the garden rather than transplanting seedlings. Zucchini germinates reliably and is easy to seed. Direct seeding is especially practical if you have a large garden because it reduces the work of caring for the transplant while it becomes established. However, the advantage to transplanting is that you buy only as many plants as you need; if you have a small garden, one plant is often enough.*

• If you do prefer to transplant zucchini, try not to disturb the roots: zucchini plants do not like to have their roots disturbed. If more than one plant is growing in your pack, do not attempt to separate them. Instead, leave them as they are, or else simply pinch out the weakest seedling.

• Zucchini is famous for its quick growth. Under warm conditions, you can be harvesting small zucchini within a week after the flowers are pollinated. If you pick the fruit while they are small, the plant will respond by producing more flowers; however, if you allow the fruit to get large, the plant will flower less prolifically. So pick small zucchini every three or four days in July and August to maintain a continuous supply of small fruit, but allow a few zucchini to grow large, particularly toward the end of the season.

• If you are harvesting flowers, avoid removing the female blooms, which produce the fruit. But be sure not to remove all the male flowers either, because you need some pollinator flowers. You can remove the flowers from the ends of baby zucchini without damaging the fruit; before the flower fades, gently break it from the tip of the young fruit. You can then use the flowers in stir-fries, salads, or other recipes (see pages 56 and 57). Male flowers have long, slender stems; female flowers are large and have very short stems.

• The best way to harvest zucchini is to cut the fruit from the plant with a sharp knife, leaving a bit of the stem. A clean cut prevents disease organisms from getting established and ensures that you do not damage the plant and its root system.

• When harvesting zucchini for storage, be sure that you leave the stem end on the fruit and that there are no nicks or cuts on the fruit (disease organisms can enter through damaged skin). If the skin is damaged, use the fruit immediately.

• To determine whether a zucchini fruit will last in storage, gently attempt to press your thumb nail through the skin. If your nail easily pierces the skin, the fruit will not keep; put it in the refrigerator and use it within a few days. If the skin is tough and you cannot pierce it, the fruit will keep for several weeks.

Cooking with Zucchini
—Chef's Notes

by John Butler

The long, arduous, yet ultimately satisfying process of constructing a cookbook on a single subject is not a challenge for the faint of heart. During my research, I found no shortage of information on the topic of zucchini, with many references to using the vegetable in unique and creative ways.

My initial concept was to develop a series of recipes using traditional cooking procedures. My aim was to expand the use of zucchini in recipes where the vegetable becomes an integral part of the composition and not just a way to "hide" zucchini.

Zucchini shows an amazing versatility for recipe development, with many attractive attributes. It has a neutral, subtle flavour and excellent colour; it is affordable, readily available, and easy to grow; and it is nutritious and can be cooked in a short time in so many creative ways. The nature of the vegetable lends itself to vegetarian-style recipes, which I found myself being drawn to as the book progressed. This trait does not mean that zucchini should not become a complement to meat, poultry, fish, and game recipes—there are many included in this book—but rather, that we should recognize the ability of this vegetable to stand on its own.

Complex projects such as this one begin with a clear vision, but without reason will take off on an entirely original tangent. My experiments with recipes became a form of alchemy, in which I blended, mixed, and combined textures and flavours to produce interesting and nutritious food. Simplicity is my primary focus, and although some recipes in this book take more time and effort than others, I have tried to minimize preparation time and complicated procedures.

The current movement in the agricultural industry toward organic farming is creating a fundamental change in culinary circles. Both the Canadian public and the countries that import Canadian products increasingly recognize that we must manage the land that supplies our food in a responsible way. This changing awareness in turn demands a fresh approach to the way we eat.

Chefs and restaurateurs also play a significant role in this process. I am gratified to watch a new generation of chefs who are willing to design recipes and menus to use locally produced foods and support farmers who are committed to raising uncontaminated food products.

Zucchini in the Kitchen

Zucchini has been used for centuries in Italian cuisine. The French adopted the vegetable and originally named it *courge d'Italie*. The common name *courgette*, used today in France and many English-speaking countries, derives from this earlier name.

For the purposes of this book, I have developed a system of weights and comparison for the zucchini called for in the recipes, as follows.

	imperial weight	metric	length
baby zucchini	½ oz.	15 g	1 inch/2.5 cm
small zucchini	3½ oz.	100 g	5–6 inches/13–15 cm
medium zucchini	6 oz.	180 g	8–9 inches/20–23 cm
large zucchini	1 lb. and up	454 g and up	12–15 inches/30–35 cm or longer

Zucchini fruits grow very quickly once they start. You will need to harvest garden zucchini at least once a week for medium and large zucchini, two or three times a week for baby and small zucchini. Remember that you can also pick and eat zucchini blossoms, which will forestall the development of fruit; however, the plant responds to picking by producing more blooms.

Choosing Zucchini

When you select zucchini at the grocery store, look for zucchini that have an even colour and smooth, shiny skin. In the garden, check the skin to ensure it is smooth, with no blemishes. Wash zucchini well to remove any dirt or chemicals; dry thoroughly but gently, and store in the refrigerator. Zucchini will keep for only a few days, so use it quickly; don't pick more than you need, or else freeze what you cannot use right away (see below).

The texture and thickness of the zucchini skin varies. Whether or not you peel the zucchini before cooking is a matter of choice; however, there are some recipes in this book that call specifically for peeled zucchini.

The moisture content of zucchini also varies. The freshest zucchini will "bleed" slightly when it is cut, and small droplets of moisture will form on the cut edge. These zucchini will be crisp, with no softness in the tissue, and are best for salads and eating raw. Older zucchini may develop a bitter flavour, and the texture of the flesh will be soft.

Grating

Three small whole zucchini yield about 2½ cups (625 mL) of grated zucchini; two medium whole zucchini yield about 3 cups (750 mL). Grated zucchini will keep for a day or two in the refrigerator in a tightly sealed container.

When I grate zucchini, I use the grating blade with the largest holes. I find that small zucchini fit well into the feeder on the food processor. Larger grated zucchini is generally easier to drain and gives a better texture to most recipes.

To draw the excess moisture out of grated zucchini, place the grated zucchini in a bowl and sprinkle with salt (2–3 tsp./10–15 mL for 4 cups/1 L of grated zucchini). Stir the mixture once or twice, then set aside for 15–45 minutes. Rinse the zucchini and drain in a strainer; if necessary, squeeze the zucchini through a single layer of cheesecloth to remove the excess moisture.

Freezing Zucchini

I usually freeze only small and medium zucchini. Here's the basic method.

1. Cut the zucchini into large dice or rounds.
2. Blanch the zucchini by immersing it in boiling water for 1 minute.
3. Immediately cool the zucchini under cold running water or in an ice-water bath until the pieces are thoroughly cold.
4. Drain the zucchini in a colander and spread the pieces on a layer of absorbent paper towel or a tea towel.
5. Pack the zucchini in usable amounts in resealable plastic freezer bags. Record the date on the bag and freeze.

Frozen zucchini can be used as a vegetable or as an addition to soups, stews, and sauces. Defrost the zucchini in the microwave oven or drop them frozen into boiling water for 2–3 minutes to thaw.

Seasoning

The addition of salt and pepper to recipes is a matter of individual taste. Unless the recipe is being made in volume, the seasonings should be added "to taste." However, for the best flavour, I recommend that you add freshly ground black pepper (unless otherwise directed) to your recipes.

Lime and lemon juice are excellent flavour additives and replace salt as a healthier alternative. They are well suited to the zucchini recipes. Serve lime and lemon wedges at the table in place of salt.

Nutritional Data

Please note that the nutritional data provided with each recipe are approximate. Many variables affect the calculation of these figures, from minute differences in measurements to the variations among prepared ingredients; therefore, the nutritional data represent only a guideline and not absolute figures. We have provided the data for your information, to make meal planning easier and to assist those people with special dietary concerns; however, these numbers do not replace the specific advice of a registered dietitian.

Notes on Pre-Preparation

I am a great believer that the enjoyment of time spent cooking is connected to the time spent preparing ingredients. This pre-preparation, or in classical kitchen terminology, *mis-en-place*, is traditionally a time to prepare specific recipe ingredients before they are cooked.

Pre-preparation can include peeling and cutting vegetables, mixing pastas and doughs, chopping and storing herbs, or making bread crumbs. Many of the recipes in this book begin with pre-preparation suggestions and then continue with the actual cooking method. This system may take some adjustment and planning, but with patience and practice, cooking will become a more enjoyable experience.

The key to a successful cooking experience is to read the recipe all the way through before you start to cook. Gather the ingredients and utensils you will need, and complete any pre-preparation steps, such as chopping or grating. Once you have the initial preparation out of the way, most recipes go together fairly quickly.

The celebrity chefs on television use pre-preparation to enable them to assemble recipes with a minimum of washing, peeling, and chopping. I like to have all the ingredients for my recipes in small dishes ready to be blended together and cooked. If I have ingredients that take the same time to cook and can be added to the recipe at the same time, I put them together on a platter to make more room on my kitchen counter.

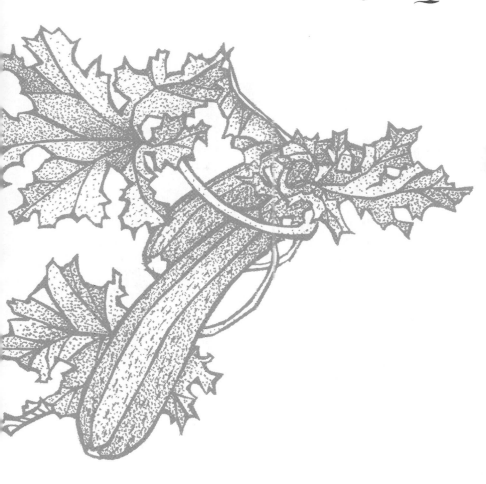

Cooking and Time Management

You can even use pre-preparation as a form of time management. In many cases, you can prepare the recipe elements hours or even days before you are ready to finish the final dish. Perhaps you have time for pre-preparation in the morning before you go to work. Do some or all of the washing, peeling, chopping, grating, and measuring when you have some extra time, then put the ingredients aside, covered, in the refrigerator or cupboard until you're ready to cook. It's a wonderful feeling at the end of the day to know that you have only a few minutes' work to put a delicious, healthy meal on the table.

You can also get your children involved in the kitchen. They can help to wash vegetables, pick fresh herbs, or measure and mix ingredients. It is a great way to teach. Share, communicate, and be patient. Make it fun, and your children will remember those precious times and thank you for them when they're grown.

Two Important Methods

The following methods can be used as the base for a number of the recipes in this book. Both also make pleasant side dishes on their own.

Barbecued Zucchini

  medium or large zucchini
  salt and pepper, or your favourite seasoning

- Start the barbecue or grill.
- Wash the zucchini and trim off the ends. Split the zucchini lengthwise.
- Hold the zucchini with the cut edge facing the palm of your hand. With a vegetable peeler, peel a strip from the bottom of the zucchini to leave a flat surface (this will prevent the zucchini from rolling). Score the flat edge of the zucchini with shallow cross marks.
- With a kitchen spoon or melon-baller, scoop out the seeds—don't scoop too deep!
- Season the zucchini with seasoning blends or lemon pepper, or stuff with your choice of filling (salsa or corn relish are great!).
- Place the zucchini on a medium-hot barbecue or grill. Cook for 5–6 minutes, or until the zucchini is tender.
- Serve hot with herb butter (see page 62).

You can also bake or broil zucchini using this method. For extra flavour, brush the zucchini with an infused oil while it's cooking.

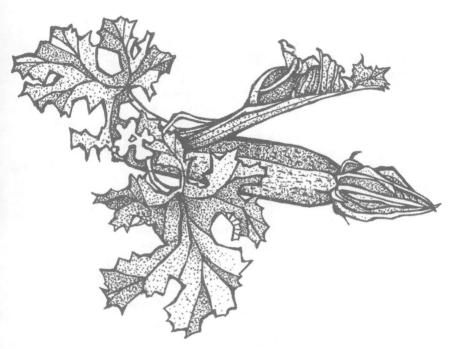

Grilled Zucchini Slices

medium or small zucchini
vegetable oil or olive oil for brushing
assorted seasonings, to taste

- Start the barbecue or grill.
- Wash the zucchini and trim the ends. Slice the zucchini lengthwise on the mandolin. The slices should be $\frac{1}{8}$ inch (0.25 cm) thick—don't slice them too thin. A medium zucchini will make about 6 slices; a small zucchini will make about 4 slices.
- Brush the slices lightly with oil and sprinkle with the seasoning of your choice, such as lemon pepper, Cajun spice mix, or Italian seasoning.
- Place the slices on the grill over high heat. Grill 3–4 minutes, turning once with tongs. Don't put too many pieces on the grill; cook a few at a time to prevent overcooking the strips.
- Drain the cooked strips on a layer of absorbent paper towel. Serve warm.

For richer flavour, you can brush the strips lightly with barbecue sauce as they cook. For a milder flavour, use infused oils or light oil-based salad dressings.

Use firm, fresh zucchini for grilling. The older the zucchini, the greater the possibility that the core will become soft after grilling. A soft core will cause the pieces to break, which will make the strips difficult to use in recipes.

Zucchini Garnishes

Not only can you enjoy zucchini in a wealth of recipes, but you can also use it as a decorative element on your table. Here are a few suggestions.

Rounds

With a small, sharp knife, slice a 2-inch (5-cm) piece of zucchini. Hollow out the centre with a melon-baller. As a variation, make one diagonal cut across the zucchini and one straight cut; this will create a round with an open diagonal face.

Rings

Cut a series of 1-inch (2-cm) slices from the zucchini. Hollow out the centres with a melon-baller to form rings. The rings can be used as holders for vegetable sticks or cooked as a decorative vegetable.

Crowns

Insert the point of a small paring knife about $1\frac{1}{2}$ inches (4 cm) from the end of the zucchini. Make a small diagonal cut. The cut should penetrate to only halfway through the zucchini (that is, only to the centre). Continue making a series of diagonal cuts until you have cut around the zucchini and the cuts join up. Gently remove the cut piece. Cut through the zucchini $1\frac{1}{2}$ inches (4 cm) from the cut edges to form a second crown. Scoop out zucchini pulp with a melon-baller.

Baskets

Cut a 3-inch (7.5 cm) section of zucchini. With a sharp paring knife, remove a small slice of the peel to form a steady base. Stand the section on the base. Form the handle of the basket by making a downward cut halfway through the section. Repeat this procedure on the other end of the section, leave a $\frac{1}{2}$-inch (1-cm) strip in the centre. From each end, make a horizontal cut toward the centre, stopping the cut on either side of the handle. Remove the pieces. Scoop out the zucchini pulp from the handle with a melon-baller and hollow out the centre of the basket to form a cavity.

Ingredients and utensils

Here is a list of foods and tools that I use in this book. Some of them may be familiar to you, while others may be new. Don't be afraid to experiment with a method or ingredient that you haven't tried before: it's the only way to discover new tastes and learn new kitchen practices.

Bamboo steamer baskets: These baskets come in a variety of sizes and can be found in Oriental grocery stores and markets. They are light and easy to store, and when the bamboo imparts a wonderful, subtle flavour to the food when it is steamed.

Bread crumbs: I make bread crumbs in my food processor from day-old white bread with the crusts left on. I package any extra crumbs in resealable plastic bags and freeze them. You can season the bread crumbs with your favourite herbs and spices for a little extra flavour.

Chayote squash: Chayote (Chay-oh-tee) is a member of the gourd family native to South America and has a delicate flavour. It can be cooked cut in half and stuffed. I like to use it in fruit and vegetable salsas for colour and crunch.

Chicken broth: I make chicken broth from the bones of roasted chicken. It takes a very short time to cook and extract the flavour from the bones. The colour is not always light as with a true chicken stock but it is a good general broth. In a pinch, canned chicken broth is adequate for most applications where a chicken stock is required.

Coconut cream: Coconut cream is the heavy residue that settles on top of coconut milk. There is also a solid bar or block of coconut cream that is sold commercially; it must be reconstituted with hot water before use.

Five-Spice Powder: This is a spice blend made from star anise, fennel, cloves, cassia, ginger, and cardamom or Sichuan pepper. I use this powder in small quantities for seasoning meat and poultry or in marinades.

Ghee (ghi): This product is often used in Indian cooking. Butter is melted and simmered until all the water has evaporated. The clarified butter takes on a slight nutty flavour. With the water and milk solids absent, the butter can be used for high temperature cooking.

Garlic: When chopping garlic add a pinch or two of salt. This will prevent the garlic from sticking to the knife blade and make it easier to chop as the salt acts as an abrasive.

Herb seasoning and blends: Commercial seasonings have found a place in my spice shelf. I prefer the types with no salt added. Used in moderation, they can add an interesting flavour to a variety of dishes.

Hot peppers: When handling hot peppers, you might choose to wear disposable gloves and must avoid touching your nose and eyes. If your mouth is burning from the heat of peppers in a dish, eat a few cucumber slices or a spoonful of plain yogourt.

Infused and flavoured vinegars: Commonly found in most grocery stores, wine and herb vinegars feature such flavours as thyme, basil, and tarragon. The flavour of fresh herbs is easily infused into vinegar. Fruits such as blueberry, strawberry, and raspberry add another range of flavours when infused with vinegar.

Japanese rice vinegar: I was introduced to the Chinese and Japanese vinegars as a flavouring for rice and vegetables. They are lighter and milder than most commercial vinegars. Some of the higher-quality vinegars of this type are made from unpolished glutinous rice.

Lemongrass: Any recipe that uses lemon as a flavouring will be enhanced by the addition of lemongrass. Only the bulb end of the stem is eaten. Use the upper leaves for infusion in steamed foods or on the barbecue to produce a lemon-scented smoke.

Mandolin: A manually operated slicer with adjustable blades for slicing, cutting matchstick shapes, or making waffle cuts.

Peeled and deveined: A reference to purchased shrimp. Often abbreviated P and D.

Panko crumbs: A coarse or large-flaked, white unseasoned Japanese bread crumb. The coating adds a crisp texture to breaded products.

Prepared sauces: I keep tomato base sauces in my kitchen. They make a good base for pizza, pasta, and some entreés, and are easy to enhance with fresh chopped tomatoes and herbs.

Roasted peppers: The best way to roast peppers is to coat them lightly with oil and roast them in a hot oven until the skin is blistered and charred. I have also used the grill or barbecue to achieve the same effect. Take the peppers and place them in a plastic bag and seal the bag. Let the peppers steam. When they are cooled, scrape away the charred skin and remove the seeds. Another method is to place the peppers in a bowl and cover with plastic wrap until the peppers are cool.

Seasoned flours: For preparation of foods to be dredged in flour, the simplest form is to season the flour with salt and pepper. Some prepared seasoned flours include cayenne pepper and dry herbs. Simple batters made with seasoned flours add interesting flavours to simple foods.

Sharp knives: Buy good knives and learn how to keep them sharp. It makes cooking a safer and more pleasurable experience.

Sea bass: A prize fish with a white solid flesh free of many small bones. It holds its shape well and has a delicate flavour. Well worth the price it commands.

Sun-dried tomatoes: Sun-dried tomatoes are tomatoes that are dried in the sun. The colour varies. The freshest ones have the brightest colour and should be soft with a strong flavour. Sun-dried tomatoes also come packed in oil (olive oil is best). Use the flavoured oil for brushing on fresh bread.

Purchasing shrimp by count: The rule is the larger the shrimp, the smaller the number in the scaled weight. For example, 10–15 per pound would be large shrimp. 40–50 per pound would be small or baby shrimp.

Sea salt: Mined salt and sea salt have different origins but are almost identical when they are purchased at the grocery store. The grind of the sea salt will determine flavour. The larger the sea salt crystals, the more "biting" the salt taste. Sea salt does have a place in the kitchen, but from a nutritional perspective, it is not significantly different from table salt.

Tempura batter: A light batter coating. The word *tempura* comes from the Portuguese *tempuras*, meaning ember days when meat is not eaten. The temperature of the oil for cooking tempura should be kept at 170°F (77°C) or above 180°F (82°C); choose a good-quality, clean vegetable oil. The food should be cut into small pieces. A popular dipping sauce for tempura is a mix of soy sauce and mirin (sweet rice wine).

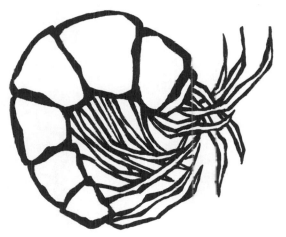

Approximate Weight-Volume Equivalents Of Common Dry Ingredients

Bread flour, sifted
1 pound = 4 cups = 1 L
4 oz. = 1 cup = 250 mL

Cake flour, sifted
1 pound = 4-1/4 cups = 1.1 L
3.75 oz. = 1 cup = 250 mL

Granulated sugar
1 pound = 2-1/4 cups = 560 mL
7 oz. = 1 cup = 250 mL

Confectioners' sugar, sifted
1 pound = 4 cups = 1 L
4 oz. = 1 cup = 250 mL

Cornstarch, unsifted
1 pound = 3-1/2 cups = 875 mL
4.5 oz. = 1 cup = 250 mL
1 oz. = 4 tbsp. = 60 mL

Cocoa, unsifted
1 pound = 5 cups = 1.3 L
3.2 oz. = 1 cup = 250 mL
1 oz. = 5 tbsp. = 75 mL

Gelatin, unflavoured
1 oz. = 3 tbsp. = 45 mL
0.11 oz = 1 tsp. = 5 mL

Baking soda and baking powder
1 oz. = 2 tbsp. = 30 mL
0.17 oz. = 1 tsp. = 5 mL

Cream of tartar
1 oz. = 4 tbsp. = 60 mL
0.08 oz. = 1 tsp. = 5 mL

Salt
1 oz. = 5 tsp. = 75 mL
0.2 oz. = 1 tsp. = 5 mL

Ground spices (except cinnamon)
1 oz. = 14 tsp. = 215 mL
0.07 oz. = 1 tsp. = 5 mL

Cinnamon
1 oz. = 17 tsp.
0.06 oz. = 1 tsp. = 5 mL

Imperial to Metric Conversion

Oven Temperatures
250°F = 120°C
275°F = 140°C
300°F = 150°C
325°F = 160°C
350°F = 180°C
375°F = 190°C
400°F = 200°C
425°F = 220°C
450°F = 230°C
475°F = 250°C
500°F = 260°C
525°F = 270°C

Volume
Pinch < 1/16 tsp.
1/16 tsp. = 0.25 mL
1/8 tsp. = 0.5 mL
1/4 tsp. = 1 mL
1/2 tsp. = 2.5 mL
1 tsp. = 5 mL
1 tbsp. = 15 mL
2 tbsp. = 30 mL
3 tbsp. = 45 mL
1/4 cup = 65 mL
1/3 cup = 85 mL
1/2 cup = 125 mL
2/3 cup = 170 mL
3/4 cup = 190 mL
1 cup = 250 mL

Length
1 inch = 25 mm

Weight
1 oz. = 30 g

Soups and Salads

Start with the Best Varieties

Zucchini is a relatively new vegetable to North American consumers. It's been widely available in Canada for about 30 years, but has really gained popularity in the last 10 to 15 years. This increasing popularity has prompted a number of seed companies to breed better varieties. We now enjoy dark-green, flecked-green, yellow, striped, and even round zucchini varieties.

Here's a list of some of the best zucchini varieties to grow.

***Super Select:** One of the most popular varieties, Super Select produces heavy yields of extra-long, dark-green fruit with light-green flecks.*

***Goldrush:** Not all zucchini varieties are green. Goldrush produces very straight, golden-yellow fruit, each an average of 20 cm long. You can treat it as a summer squash if you're picking it young; otherwise, harvest it just before the first hard frost of the fall. Mature Goldrush fruits store well, lasting a few months.*

***Spacemiser:** This outstanding variety is about five years old, and it's one of the best introductions in years. Spacemiser is a prolific plant, producing more fruit than most other varieties. It has an open growth habit, making the high-quality fruits easy to pick. Spacemiser plants have a compact growing habit, requiring less space than other varieties—great for home gardens and the best choice for containers! The fruit colours up and develops a good shape when it's very young, so this is an outstanding variety for gourmet baby squash.*

Zucchini-Leek Soup

Makes 6 servings

*Nutritional data per 290-g serving: Calories 140; fat 8 g;
sodium 1040 mg; carbohydrates 15 g; dietary fibre 2 g.*

2	small leeks, finely diced	2
1	small yellow onion, peeled and finely diced	1
3	small zucchini, diced	3
2 tbsp.	sour cream	30 mL
1 tbsp.	chopped chives	15 mL
2 tbsp.	vegetable oil	30 mL
2	medium potatoes, peeled and finely diced	2
4 cups	chicken stock	1 L
2 tsp.	chopped fresh thyme	10 mL
	salt and black pepper, to taste	

- Dice the vegetables and set them aside in separate bowls.
- Mix sour cream and chopped chives; refrigerate.
- Heat the oil in a large saucepan over medium heat. Add the leeks and onion. Cook 4–5 minutes, stirring constantly to prevent vegetables from colouring. (Adjust heat if necessary.)
- Add the potatoes and cook for 2 minutes more. Add 1 cup (250 mL) chicken stock. Bring to a boil. Add another 1 cup (250 mL) of chicken stock. Add thyme and season with salt and pepper; reduce heat to simmer. Cook 7–8 minutes, until the potatoes are almost cooked through.
- Add the zucchini and the remaining chicken stock; cook for 5 minutes over low heat. Check seasoning.
- Serve hot with a dollop of the sour cream–chive mix on top of each bowl.

Chef's notes: If you substitute dried thyme for fresh, add only half the amount indicated. • Serve this soup with fresh baguette, Italian bread, or herb focaccia. Garnish with seasoned bread croutons.

Zucchini Minestrina

Makes 4–6 servings

Nutritional data per 350-g serving: Calories 300; fat 14 g; sodium 1110 mg; carbohydrates 35 g; dietary fibre 8 g.

4 tbsp.	olive oil	60 mL
5	garlic cloves, minced	5
1	small yellow onion, peeled and finely diced	1
2 cups	chopped green cabbage	500 mL
4 cups	chicken stock	1 L
1 cup	dry baby shell pasta (conchigliette)	250 mL
1 cup	canned garbanzo beans, drained	250 mL
1 cup	canned plum tomatoes, chopped, with juice	250 mL
2	small zucchini, diced	2
2 tbsp.	chopped fresh parsley	30 mL
½ tbsp.	chopped fresh thyme	7.5 mL
	salt and black pepper to taste	

- Heat oil in a large saucepan over medium heat; add garlic. Cook quickly; do not let the garlic burn.
- Add the onion and cabbage. Cook, stirring, until the onions and cabbage are soft, about 5–6 minutes. Adjust heat if necessary.
- Add the chicken stock and pasta; bring to a simmer. Add the garbanzo beans and tomatoes plus juice. Add the zucchini; cook for 2 minutes at a gentle boil. Add the parsley and thyme. Season to taste.
- Serve hot.

Chef's notes: In her book *Essentials of Italian Cooking*, Marcella Hazan calls soup like this *minestrina,* or "little soup." • Serve this soup over toasted bread brushed with olive oil and sprinkled with Parmesan cheese. Place bread in the bottom of soup bowls and pour the hot soup over it. • Serve pesto or freshly grated Parmesan cheese at the table to accompany this fresh-flavoured soup. • Add baby shrimp or baby clams to the soup as a garnish.

Zucchini-Coconut-Curry Soup

Makes 3½ cups (875 mL)

Nutritional data per 275-g serving: Calories 350; fat 33 g; sodium 40 mg; carbohydrates 15 g, dietary fibre 4 g.

1 tbsp.	peanut oil	15 mL
1	small yellow onion, finely diced	1
2 tsp.	hot curry paste	10 mL
2	medium celery stalks, finely ciced	2
1	medium zucchini, finely diced	1
1	small apple, cored, peeled, and finely diced	1
	salt and pepper, to taste	
14-oz. can	coconut milk	398-mL can
	sweet mango chutney, to taste	
	toasted desiccated coconut	

- Heat the oil in a heavy, medium-sized saucepan over medium heat. Add the onion and celery; cook, stirring constantly, until the vegetables are softened, about 4–5 minutes.
- Remove from heat and add the curry paste. Return to heat and cook 1 minute.
- Add the zucchini and apple; cook, stirring occasionally, until the apple and zucchini are soft, about 3–4 minutes. Season lightly
- Add the coconut milk and bring to a simmer. Reduce heat; cook gently 4–5 minutes.
- Serve hot, garnished with mango chutney and coconut.

Chef's notes: For extra flair, garnish soup with chopped cilantro and serve with fresh lime wedges.

Zucchini Blender Gazpacho

Makes 5 cups (1.3 L)

Nutritional data per 300-g serving: Calories 230; fat 14 g; sodium 1110 mg; carbohydrates 23 g; dietary fibre 3 g.

3 tbsp.	olive oil	45 mL
2 tbsp.	balsamic vinegar	30 mL
2	garlic cloves	2
3 cups	tomato juice	750 mL
1 cup	canned plum tomatoes, drained	250 mL
1	small cucumber, peeled, seeded, and diced	1
3	small celery stalks, diced	3
1	small red onion, peeled and diced	1
8 sprigs	parsley	8 sprigs
1	small zucchini, grated	1
2 tsp.	lemon juice	10 mL
	salt and black pepper, to taste	

- In the blender jar, combine the olive oil, balsamic vinegar, and garlic. Add 1 cup (250 mL) of tomato juice; blend until the garlic is chopped.
- Add ½ cup (125 mL) of the plum tomatoes, plus the cucumber, celery, onion, and parsley; blend until ingredients are puréed.
- Pour mixture into a non-corrosive bowl and refrigerate.
- Pour the remaining 2 cups (500 mL) of tomato juice in the blender jar. Add the zucchini and lemon juice; blend.
- Pour this mixture into the refrigerated mixture. Season, cover, and refrigerate for at least 2 hours.
- Serve cold in chilled bowls.

Chef's notes: Garnish soup with additional grated zucchini or small bread croutons. • Cold soups should be overseasoned. If the soup tastes acidic or bitter, add a teaspoon of sugar with the seasoning. Add a few drops of hot pepper sauce or Worcestershire sauce for additional flavour.

Zucchini and Onion Salad

Makes 5 servings

Nutritional data per 120-g serving: Calories 90; fat 5 g; sodium 350 mg; carbohydrates 12 g; dietary fibre 1 g.

2	small zucchini, thinly sliced	2
1	small red onion, thinly sliced	1
1 tbsp.	chopped fresh dill	15 mL
½ cup	sour cream	125 mL
⅓ cup	malt vinegar	85 mL
3 tbsp.	sugar	45 mL
1 tbsp.	grainy Dijon mustard	15 mL
	salt and pepper, to taste	

- In a medium glass bowl, mix together the zucchini, onion, and dill.
- In a separate bowl, combine the sour cream, malt vinegar, sugar, mustard, salt, and pepper. Mix well.
- Just before serving, combine all ingredients. (The ingredients can be prepared in advance and kept tightly sealed in the refrigerator until you need the salad.)

Chef's notes: This recipe makes a great side salad with fresh bread. • Served over sliced tomatoes with lots of freshly ground black pepper or over mixed greens. • Try it as a wrap filling with shredded lettuce and diced tomatoes.

Grilled Zucchini Salad

Makes 4 servings

Nutritional data per 200-g serving: Calories 270; fat 26g; sodium 950 mg; carbohydrates 9 g; dietary fibre 3 g.

3	small zucchini, cut in diagonal strips and grilled	3
1	small red onion, finely diced	1
½	medium red pepper, finely diced	½
12	pitted green olives, chopped	12
12	pitted black olives, chopped	12
8	large fresh basil leaves, chopped	8
1 tbsp.	capers, drained	15 mL
⅓ cup	extra-virgin olive oil	85 mL
1 tbsp.	lemon juice	15 mL
	salt and black pepper, to taste	

- Grill the zucchini strips using the method on page 25.
- Place the grilled zucchini in a large ceramic or glass bowl. Add the diced onion, red pepper, and olives; mix lightly with a wooden spoon. The zucchini will be soft, so do not overmix.
- Add the basil and capers. Add lemon juice and olive oil; mix lightly. Season to taste.
- Serve salad over crisp mixed greens with fresh bread.

Chef's notes: Another serving idea is to layer the grilled strips on flour tortillas and top with salad greens or your preferred hot filling.

Did you know...?

The International Zucchini Festival is held every August in Harrisville, New Hampshire.

Grated Zucchini Salad

Makes 4 servings

Nutritional data per 200-g serving: Calories 190; fat 16 g; sodium 730 mg; carbohydrates 9 g; dietary fibre 4 g.

3	small zucchini, grated	3
1 tsp.	salt	10 mL
½ cup	sour cream	125 mL
⅓ cup	mayonnaise	85 mL
2 tsp.	lemon juice	10 mL
2 tbsp.	chopped chives	30 mL
1	small red pepper, finely diced	1
2	medium celery stalks, finely diced	2
⅓ cup	frozen baby peas, defrosted	85 mL
	salt and black pepper, to taste	

- In a medium bowl, mix together grated zucchini and salt. Let stand for 45 minutes. Strain the zucchini through a single layer of cheesecloth and squeeze out the excess liquid.
- In a separate medium bowl, mix together sour cream, mayonnaise, lemon juice, and chives.
- Add the strained zucchini to the sour cream-mayonnaise mix. Stir in the peppers, celery, and peas; mix gently.
- Season with salt and pepper; serve over fresh greens.

Chef's notes: You can use light sour cream or plain yogourt in place of the sour cream. You can also replace the mayonnaise with light mayonnaise.

Cool Corn Salad

Makes 6 servings

*Nutritional data per 160-g serving: Calories 180; fat 14 g;
sodium 280 mg; carbohydrates 12 g; dietary fibre 3 g.*

12-oz. can	canned kernel corn, drained	340-mL can
2	small zucchini, finely diced	2
8	cherry tomatoes	8
2 tbsp.	chopped fresh parsley	30 mL
2 tsp.	chopped fresh tarragon	10 mL
1 tbsp.	grain mustard	15 mL
1 tsp.	brown sugar	5 mL
1 tbsp.	white-wine vinegar	15 mL
1 tbsp.	sweet chili sauce	15 mL
	tabasco sauce, to taste	
	freshly ground black pepper, to taste	
⅓ cup	safflower oil	85 mL

• In a large bowl, mix the drained corn with the zucchini.

• Quarter the cherry tomatoes and add to the bowl gently.

• Add the parsley, tarragon, grain mustard, and brown sugar; mix gently.

• Add the white-wine vinegar, chili sauce, and a few drops of tabasco sauce.
Season with pepper. Add the safflower oil and gently toss the salad.

• Cover salad and refrigerate 2–3 hours before serving.

Chef's notes: This makes an excellent summer salad, or serve it on the side with grilled meats and chicken. • Replace the fresh tarragon with 1 tsp. (5 mL) of dried tarragon if necessary.

Zucchini and Jicama Salad

Makes 4 servings

*Nutritional data per 200-g serving: Calories 275; fat 13 g;
sodium 550 mg; carbohydrates 9 g; dietary fibre 5 g.*

3	small zucchini	3
2 cups	jicama, peeled and cut into small batons	500 mL
¼ cup	vegetable oil	65 mL
2 tbsp.	lime juice	30 mL
2 tsp.	chopped fresh cilantro	10 mL
	salt and pepper, to taste	
	fresh lettuce leaves or salad greens	

- Wash the zucchini and cut into small batons.
- Peel the jicama and slice into small batons.
- Combine the vegetables into a medium bowl; pour the vegetable oil and lime juice over them.
- Add the chopped cilantro, and season with salt and pepper. Toss all ingredients to mix well. Refrigerate for 1 hour. Toss the mixture every 20 minutes to incorporate all the flavours.
- Serve over lettuce leaves.

Chef's notes: For best flavour, use small, absolutely fresh zucchini. • This recipe works well with chayote in place of the jicama. • For an added touch, serve this dish with fresh mandarin orange segments.

Southwestern Salad

Makes 4–6 servings

Nutritional data per 310-g serving: Calories 200; fat 12 g; sodium 520 mg; carbohydrates 22 g; dietary fibre 4 g.

4	small zucchini, finely diced	4
3	Roma tomatoes, finely diced	3
1 cup	canned kernel corn, drained	250 mL
1	medium red onion, finely diced	1
1	avocado, finely diced	1
1 tbsp.	lime juice	15 mL
4	green onions, chopped	4
1 tbsp.	chopped fresh cilantro	15 mL
2 tbsp.	vegetable oil	30 mL
1 cup	medium-hot salsa	250 mL
	black pepper, to taste	

- In a large bowl, mix together the zucchini, tomatoes, corn, and red onion.
- In a medium bowl, mix together the avocado, lime juice, green onion, cilantro, vegetable oil, and salsa. Mix well.
- Combine the avocado mix with the zucchini mix in the large bowl; mix well. Season with black pepper. Cover with plastic wrap and refrigerate for 4 hours.
- Serve as a side salad or over mixed greens.

Did you know...?

Zucchini is a good source of Vitamin K.

Garden Vegetable Salad

Makes 4 servings

Nutritional data per 530-g serving: Calories 530; fat 21 g; sodium 410 mg; carbohydrates 74 g, dietary fibre 13 g.

8	baby red potatoes	8
2	small zucchini, cut into medium dice	2
½ lb.	green beans, sliced	250 g
½ cup	canned red kidney beans, rinsed and drained	125 mL
2	garlic cloves, crushed	2
⅓ cup	olive oil	85 mL
2 tbsp.	white-wine vinegar	30 mL
2 tsp.	granulated sugar	10 mL
2 tbsp.	Dijon mustard	30 mL
1	large carrot, grated	1
½ lb.	mixed salad greens	250 g

- Cook the potatoes whole in salted water for 10 minutes. Cool and cut into quarters; set aside.
- Steam the zucchini and green beans for 5–6 minutes. Refresh under cold water; set aside.
- In a medium bowl, combine the garlic, olive oil, white-wine vinegar, sugar, and Dijon mustard; mix well.
- Mix all the vegetables together; pour the dressing over top. Toss together until well mixed. Cover and refrigerate for 1 hour.
- Garnish with grated carrot and serve over salad greens.

Chef's notes: For extra flavour, add a sprig of mint to the potato water.

Zucchini and Spinach, Italian Style

Makes 4 servings

Nutritional data per 235-g serving: Calories 320; fat 30 g;
sodium 790 mg; carbohydrates 8 g; dietary fibre 3 g

½ cup	olive oil	125 mL
4	small zucchini, cut into batons	4
4	garlic cloves, crushed	4
1	large bunch spinach, cleaned and stemmed	1
2 tsp.	fresh thyme	10 mL
8	fresh basil leaves	8
	salt and pepper, to taste	
3	Roma tomatoes, finely diced	3
½ cup	grated Parmesan cheese	125 mL

• Heat the olive oil in a large skillet over high heat. When the oil is hot, add the zucchini batons and toss in the oil until they are golden-brown. Remove the batons from the oil, drain on paper towel, and keep warm.

• Reduce heat to medium and add the garlic to the skillet. Add the spinach; cook until tender. Add the thyme and basil; cook for 3 minutes. Season with salt and pepper.

• Divide the cooked spinach among 4 small plates. Top with the reserved zucchini batons. Sprinkle with diced tomatoes and Parmesan cheese.

• Serve warm with fresh Italian bread.

Appetizers and Side Dishes

Growing Zucchini

Zucchini is a summer squash. Like all summer squashes, it requires rich, well-drained soil with a pH of 6.5–7.5 and a sunny, sheltered place to grow. Leave plenty of room for each plant; all zucchini plants have a bush growth habit, covering up to 1.5 square metres of ground. (The compact variety 'Spacemiser' covers about 0.9 square metres.)

Zucchini plants are tender and easily damaged by frost, so sow seed or transplant seedlings into the garden well after all danger of frost has passed. Soil temperatures should be at least 15°C for germination; optimum soil temperature for germination is 21–35°C. If the soil temperature is 30–35°C, plants can emerge in less than a week. After germination, zucchini grows best at the height of summer, when temperatures are in the range of 18–24°C. Growth stops if temperatures dip below 10°C.

Plant zucchini seeds every 30 cm for best results, planting to a depth of about 2 cm. For an earlier harvest, start seeds indoors about two weeks prior to planting or purchase young plants from a greenhouse. Once the plants are growing well, thin to leave a 60-cm space between plants. Since zucchini produces so heavily, yielding about 16 fruit per plant, 2 to 4 plants will provide sufficient quantities for an average family.

Zucchini requires little care in the garden. Zucchini plants have good drought tolerance thanks to their deep root systems (although not as deep as winter squash), but even so, their fruit require plenty of moisture, especially to prevent conditions like blossom-end rot (see page 80). During dry weather, give the plants a good soaking once per week, early in the day so that the plants will dry before nightfall; wet plants at night invite disease. Avoid splashing dirt on the leaves when you water; this is how soil-borne diseases infect foliage.

Zucchini plants produce both male and female flowers, the male flowers usually appearing earlier in the season than the female blooms. Don't worry about pollination; insects will tackle the job.

Zucchini Bites

Makes 8–10 portions

Nutritional data per 67-g serving: Calories 73; fat 2 g; sodium 106 mg; carbohydrates 12 g, dietary fibre 1 g.

2 cups	grated zucchini	500 mL
1	large egg, beaten	1
⅔ cup	all-purpose flour	165 mL
⅓ cup	cornmeal	85 mL
1	small yellow onion, grated	1
1 tsp.	dried basil	5 mL
	salt and pepper, to taste	
2 tsp.	baking powder	10 mL
	vegetable oil for frying	

- In a medium bowl, mix together the zucchini, beaten egg, flour, cornmeal, grated onion, basil, salt, and pepper. Add the baking powder.
- Heat the oil to 350°F.
- With a teaspoon, carefully spoon the mixture into the hot oil. Cook pieces until they are golden-brown.
- Remove bites with a slotted spoon and drain on paper towel. Serve hot.

Zucchini Toasts

Makes about 24 toasts

Nutritional data per 30-g serving: Calories 110; fat 3 g;
sodium 190 mg; carbohydrates 4 g; dietary fibre 1 g.

2 cups	grated zucchini	500 mL
2 tsp.	salt	10 mL
½ cup	mayonnaise	125 mL
½ cup	sour cream	125 mL
2 tbsp.	grated Romano cheese	30 mL
½	red pepper, finely diced	½
2	medium stalks celery, finely diced	2
2	green onions, diced	2
2 drops	Tabasco sauce	2 drops
	salt and pepper to taste	
24-inch	baguette	60-cm
2 tbsp.	olive oil	30 mL

- Place the grated zucchini in a glass bowl. Sprinkle with salt and let stand at room temperature for 1 hour.
- In a medium bowl, mix the mayonnaise, sour cream, Romano cheese, red pepper, celery, green onions, Tabasco sauce, salt, and pepper. Mix well.
- Drain the zucchini through a single layer of cheesecloth, squeezing out all the excess moisture. Stir into the mayonnaise-yogourt mix.
- Slice the baguette into rounds 1 inch (2.5 cm) thick. Place on a bake sheet. Brush with rounds olive oil and toast under the broiler on both sides until golden-brown. Cool the toasts.
- Place a spoonful of the mixture on each toast round and bake at 375°F (190°C) for 8–10 minutes.

Chef's notes: You can also use light rye, foccacia, or whole-wheat bread in place of the baguette. • For a larger portion, the zucchini mix can be placed on a hamburger bun instead of baguette rounds. • You can replace the sour cream with light sour cream or yogourt. • For an extra topping, sprinkle the filling with grated Parmesan cheese and broil.

Zucchini-Stuffed Mushrooms

Makes 4 servings

Nutritional data per 290-g serving: Calories 190; fat 7 g; sodium 230 mg; carbohydrates 29 g; dietary fibre 4 g.

2	large portabella mushrooms	2
	or	
4	large field mushrooms	4
2 tsp.	olive oil	10 mL
2	shallots, finely diced	2
½	green pepper, finely diced	½
½	red pepper, finely diced	½
½ cup	grated zucchini	125 mL
1 tsp.	grated lemon rind	5 mL
1 tbsp.	chopped fresh thyme	15 mL
2 tbsp.	chopped fresh parsley	30 mL
1 tbsp.	red wine	15 mL
1 cup	bread crumbs	250 mL
2 tbsp.	ketchup	30 mL
1	large egg, beaten	1
	salt and pepper, to taste	
2 tbsp.	grated Parmesan cheese	30 mL
1 tsp.	olive oil	5 mL

- Preheat oven to 350°F (175°C).
- Remove mushroom stems and clean caps with a damp towel. Lightly score the bases of the mushrooms with a small, sharp knife.
- Heat 2 tsp. (10 mL) olive oil in a medium skillet over medium heat. Add the shallots and peppers; cook for 2–3 minutes, stirring to prevent browning.
- Add the zucchini, lemon rind, thyme, and parsley. Cook for 1 minute, stirring.
- Add the red wine; cook for 1 minute. Remove from heat and cool.
- In a large bowl, mix the bread crumbs with the cooled vegetables. Add the ketchup and beaten egg. Season with salt and pepper; mix well.
- Fill the cavities of the mushrooms with stuffing. Sprinkle with Parmesan cheese; drizzle with 1 tsp. (5 mL) olive oil. Transfer mushrooms to baking sheet.
- Bake 15–20 minutes. Serve hot.

Chef's notes: To broil, place the stuffed mushrooms on a baking sheet on the middle rack of the oven. Broil 8–10 minutes, until the mushrooms are soft to the touch. • To grill, use medium-hot heat on the barbecue or grill. Do not let the mushrooms get too dry.

Deep-Fried Zucchini

Makes 4 servings

Nutritional data per 90-g serving: Calories 320; fat 29 g;
sodium 440 mg; carbohydrates 12 g; dietary fibre 1 g.

2 cups	fresh white bread crumbs	500 mL
¼ tsp.	paprika	1 mL
pinch	nutmeg	pinch
⅓ cup	grated Parmesan cheese	85 mL
2	large eggs	2
4	small zucchini, cut into slices or batons	4
2 cups	olive oil	500 mL
1	lemon, cut into wedges	1

- In a large bowl, mix together bread crumbs, paprika, nutmeg and cheese.
- In a medium bowl, beat the eggs with a whisk.
- Dip the cut zucchini in the egg mixture, then roll in the bread crumbs.
- Spread the breaded pieces on a platter. Don't stack them or they will stick together.
- Heat the oil to 325°F (160°C).
- Carefully fry the breaded pieces until they are golden-brown. Drain on paper towels, then serve with a squeeze of lemon juice. Serve with lemon wedges on the side.

Chef's notes: You can make seasoned bread crumbs ahead of time and keep them frozen in a sealed plastic bag. Here are a few seasoning suggestions: thyme, basil, and oregano; dried chili flakes and shredded coconut; chili powder; lemon pepper.

Did you know...?

A zucchini fruit is 95% water.

Zucchini-Wrapped Scallops

Makes 4 servings

*Nutritional data per 75-g serving: Calories 70; fat 0 g;
sodium 450 mg; carbohydrates 3 g; dietary fibre 1 g.*

12	large scallops	12
1 tbsp.	fresh lemon or lime juice	15 mL
2 tsp.	paprika pepper	10 mL
	salt and pepper to taste	
2	small zucchini	2
2 tbsp.	oil	30 mL

- Marinate scallops in lime or lemon juice, paprika, salt, and pepper for 30 minutes.
- With a mandolin, cut the zucchini into 12 slices ⅛ inch (0.25 cm) thick. Grill zucchini strips using the method on page 25; set aside to cool.
- Wrap each scallop in a zucchini strip and thread onto an 8-inch (20-cm) metal or bamboo skewer. Secure the end of the zucchini strip with the skewer and push the scallops lightly together to secure them. Put 3 scallops on each skewer.
- Cook the skewered scallops on a medium-high part of the grill or barbecue. Brush each skewer lightly with oil and cook for 3–4 minutes.
- With tongs, turn the skewers diagonally and brush with oil. Cook for another 3–4 minutes.
- Remove to a cooler part of the grill and cook for a further 4–5 minutes. Do not overcook.
- Serve immediately.

Chef's notes: For variety, you can use 15 to 21 count shrimp in place of the scallops. • Pelley Bay scallops are excellent if you can find them.

Tempura Zucchini Blossoms

Makes 12 servings

*Nutritional data per 15-g serving: Calories 75; fat 8 g;
sodium 15 mg; carbohydrates 2 g; dietary fibre 1 g.*

12	zucchini blossoms	12
1	large egg, beaten	1
1 cup	*cold* water	250 mL
2 tbsp.	dry white wine	30 mL
1 cup	all-purpose flour	250 mL
2 cups	peanut oil or vegetable oil	500 mL

- Wash the blossoms quickly under cold water. If stems are long, trim to 2 inches (5 cm). Larger blossoms can be butterflied by making a cut in the base to open the flower and lay it flat.
- In a medium bowl, beat the egg, cold water, and wine. Add the flour all at once and mix quickly with a whisk. Don't overmix.
- Heat the oil in a deep-fryer or wok to 340–350°F (170°C). Drop a small amount of batter into the oil to test; it should cook in about 30 seconds.
- Dip each blossom in the batter. Lower the battered blossoms into the hot oil (no more than 2 at a time) and fry for 60–90 seconds. Remove fried blossoms from oil with a slotted spoon; drain on paper towel.
- Serve hot.

Chef's notes: Tempura is traditionally served with a dipping sauce made from soy sauce, mirin, dashi, grated daikon and grated ginger.

Stuffed Zucchini Blossoms

Makes 4 servings

Nutritional data per 270-g serving: Calories 250; fat 10 g; sodium 1300 mg; carbohydrates 30 g; dietary fibre 4 g.

8	zucchini blossoms	8
2 tbsp.	olive oil	30 mL
2	garlic cloves, chopped	2
1	small red onion, finely diced	1
3	small zucchini, finely diced	3
⅓ cup	dry white wine	85 mL
2 cups	fresh white bread crumbs	500 mL
2 tbsp.	chopped fresh flat-leaf parsley	30 mL
	pinch of nutmeg	
1	large egg	1
½ cup	chicken broth	125 mL
	butter for casserole dish	
	salt and pepper to taste	

- Wash the zucchini blossoms in water; drain on paper towel and set aside.
- Preheat oven to 350°F.
- Heat olive oil in a medium skillet over medium heat. Add the garlic and cook, stirring constantly to prevent burning. Add the onion; cook for 2 minutes, until onion is soft. Add the diced zucchini; cook for 3 minutes, until soft. Add the white wine and cook for 1 minute. Remove pan from heat.
- In a medium bowl, mix the bread crumbs, parsley, nutmeg, and egg. Add the vegetable mix to the bread crumbs; mix well. If the mixture is too dry, add a small amount of chicken broth to moisten, but do not make the mixture too wet.
- Open the zucchini flowers. Remove the pistil with scissors or a small sharp knife; be careful not to damage the flower.
- Spoon some filling into each flower. Close the petals around the filling and gently twist the tops to seal.
- Butter a small casserole dish and place the blossoms in the dish. Season with salt and pepper. Pour the chicken broth into the casserole. Cover the dish and bake for 12–15 minutes.

Chef's notes: A mild-flavoured filling is appropriate for zucchini blossoms. • The blossoms are very delicate and perishable. The male blossoms attached to the stem are the best for eating. • If you find blossoms with small zucchini attached, prepare as above. The small zucchini make a nice addition to the plate.

Shrimp Wraps

Makes 4 servings

Nutritional data per 130-g serving: Calories 90; fat 4 g; sodium 420 mg; carbohydrates 4 g; dietary fibre 1 g.

8	large shrimp, peeled and deveined	8
8	scallops	8
2 tbsp.	lime juice	30 mL
2	medium zucchini	2
1 tbsp.	oil	15 mL
1 tbsp.	Italian seasoning	15 mL
	oil for grilling	
	lime wedges, for garnish	

- Set 4 8-inch (20-cm) bamboo skewers in water to soak for 30 minutes.
- In a medium bowl, combine the shrimp and scallops with lime juice; set aside to marinate.
- Cut the zucchini into lengthwise slices about ⅛ inch (0.25 cm) thick. Brush the slices with 1 tbsp. (15 mL) oil and sprinkle with seasoning. Grill using the method on page 25.
- Place the grilled slices on a flat surface to cool; they should be pliable but not fragile.
- Place a shrimp on a grilled zucchini slice; roll the shrimp inside the slice. Use the skewer to secure the loose end and slide the wrap onto the skewer.
- Repeat this rolling step with a scallop, then a shrimp, and so on. You can fit 4 wraps on 1 skewer: 2 shrimp, 2 scallops.
- Place the skewers on a medium-hot part of the barbecue for 7–8 minutes. Brush with oil if necessary, and turn once or twice.
- Garnish with fresh lime wedges and serve hot.

Chef's notes: This dish pairs well with rice. • When the barbecue season is over, you can make these wraps in the oven. Broil them on the middle rack in a glass casserole dish for 12-15 minutes, turning once • If you have small shrimp and scallops, use small zucchini. • For variety, replace the Italian seasoning with lemon pepper or paprika pepper.

Spring Rolls

Makes 8–10 rolls

*Nutritional data per 180-g serving: Calories 210; fat 14 g;
sodium 115 mg; carbohydrates 3 g; dietary fibre 2 g.*

8 to 10	spring-roll wrappers	8 to 10
1 tbsp.	sesame oil	15 mL
2	small celery stalks, cut into short lengths	2
3	green onions, chopped	3
2 tsp.	finely chopped ginger root	10 mL
1	small onion, thinly sliced	1
2	garlic cloves, crushed	2
½ cup	ground pork	125 mL
½ cup	baby shrimp, drained	125 mL
½ cup	grated zucchini	125 mL
4	field mushrooms, thinly sliced	4
1 tbsp.	soy sauce	15 mL
2 tsp.	5-spice powder	10 mL
1	egg	1
1	egg white	1
	oil for deep frying	

- Separate the spring-roll wrappers and cover with a damp towel.
- Heat sesame oil in a medium skillet. Combine the celery, green onion, ginger root, sliced onion, and garlic; cook for 3-4 minutes. Remove from heat and allow to cool.
- In a medium bowl, mix together the ground pork, shrimp, zucchini, mushrooms, soy sauce, 5-spice powder, and egg; mix well.
- Add the cooled vegetables to the meat mixture; mix well.
- In a small bowl, beat the egg white until foamy; set aside.
- Set out the spring-roll wrappers (2 at a time) in a diamond pattern.
- Place a small amount of the mixture on the bottom corner of the wrapper. Brush the outside and top edges of the wrapper with the egg white. Fold the outside corners towards the middle and roll the wrapper to enclose the filling. Repeat with remaining wrappers until all the filling is used.
- Heat oil to 350°F (170°C). Fry rolls 3-4 minutes, until lightly golden-brown; drain on paper towel.
- Serve warm with dipping sauce, soy sauce, or plain rice.

Festive Spring Rolls

Makes 4 servings

Nutritional data per 250-g serving: Calories 350; fat 6 g;
sodium 1010 mg; carbohydrates 68 g; dietary fibre 6 g.

12 8-inch	spring-roll wrappers	12 20-cm
1 cup	grated zucchini	250 mL
½ cup	baby shrimp, chopped	125 mL
1	medium carrot, grated	1
6	mushrooms, sliced	6
4	green onions, chopped	4
¼ cup	water chestnuts, chopped	65 mL
¼ cup	bamboo shoots	65 mL
2 oz.	grated ginger root	60 g
1 tsp.	5-spice powder	5 mL
	salt and pepper, to taste	
1	egg white	1
	vegetable oil for frying	

- Separate the spring-roll wrappers and cover with a damp towel.
- In a large bowl, mix together the zucchini, shrimp, carrot, mushrooms, green onions, water chestnuts, bamboo shoots, ginger root, and 5-spice powder. Add the egg and mix well; season to taste.
- In a small bowl, beat the egg white until foamy; set aside.
- Place a small amount of the filling on the bottom corner of a spring-roll wrapper. Brush the outside and top edges of the wrapper with the egg white. Fold the outside corners towards the middle and roll the wrapper to enclose the filling. Repeat with remaining wrappers until all the filling is used.
- Heat oil to 350°F (175°C). Fry rolls 3–4 minutes, until golden-brown; drain on paper towel.
- Serve with dipping sauce. Plum, teriyaki, sweet soy, or sweet chili sauce are all good choices.

Zucchini Pastries

Makes 4–6 servings

*Nutritional data per 280-g serving: Calories 450; fat 29 g;
sodium 450 mg; carbohydrates 31 g; dietary fibre 3 g.*

1 sheet	frozen prepared puff pastry	1 sheet
1 tbsp.	olive oil	15 mL
10	chopped fresh basil leaves	10
1	medium red onion, thinly sliced	1
4	small zucchini, thinly sliced	4
4	Roma tomatoes, sliced	4
2 tsp.	chili flakes	10 mL
1 cup	grated mozzarella cheese	250 mL
½ cup	grated Parmesan cheese	125 mL

- Preheat oven to 400°F (200°C).
- Place the frozen puff pastry on a cookie sheet. Brush the pastry with olive oil and sprinkle with basil.
- Cover the pastry with an even layer of onion. Cover onion layer with a layer of zucchini slices. Cover the zucchini layer with a layer of tomato slices. Sprinkle chili flakes over the layers.
- Spread the mozzarella and Parmesan over the layers. Bake pastries on the lowest oven rack until the vegetables are cooked and the pastry is crisp.
- Cut into squares or triangles, and serve.

Chef's notes: These pastries are delicious with a mixed green salad.

Steamed Zucchini Rings

Makes 4–6 servings

Nutritional data per 165-g serving: Calories 10; fat 0 g;
sodium 0 mg; carbohydrates 2 g; dietary fibre 1 g

2	medium zucchini	2
2 cups	water	500 mL
	fresh herbs for infusion (see below)	

- Wash the zucchini and trim the ends.
- With the large end of a melon-baller, remove the core and seeds from the center of the zucchini. You may not be able to hollow the zucchini all the way through; scoop as far as you can comfortably reach.
- Slice the hollowed zucchini into ½-inch (1-cm) rings. (If necessary, cut off enough rings to allow you to finish scooping out the centre.)
- Place the rings in a nested steamer basket or double boiler. Pour the water and fresh herbs in the bottom part of the steamer; bring a boil over medium high heat.
- Reduce heat to a simmer and steam the zucchini rings 5-6 minutes, until the rings are tender but not overcooked. Serve hot.

Amounts of fresh herbs for infusion

basil: 10 leaves; Thai basil: 6 leaves; mint: 8 leaves; tarragon: 1 stem; oregano: 4 stems; thyme: 2 sprigs; lemon grass: 1 stem, coarsely chopped

Chef's notes: Serve zucchini rings with fresh lime and lemon wedges, or with plain yogourt. • Make herb butters to serve with zucchini rings and other dishes. Combine 1 lb. (450 g) of unsalted butter with 2–3 tbsp. (30–45 mL) finely chopped fresh herbs; mix well. Shape the butter into attractive pats or pipe into rosettes. Store herb butters in resealable plastic bags in the freezer. • With this dish, offer herb butter at the table, or melt the butter in a sauté pan and toss the zucchini in it before serving.

Steamed Baby Zucchini

Makes 4 servings

Nutritional data per 150-g serving: Calories 190; fat 19 g;
sodium 780 mg; carbohydrates 4 g; dietary fibre 0 g.

30	baby zucchini	30
	water for steaming	
	fresh herbs for infusion (see below)	
½ cup	melted butter	125 mL
	salt and pepper, to taste	
	fresh lemon juice (optional)	

- Place the zucchini in a nested steamer basket. Don't crowd them.
- Bring the water for steaming to a boil; add any herbs for infusion.
- Steam the baby zucchini for 6–7 minutes. Check for doneness—they should be crisply firm.
- Transfer the zucchini to a serving bowl and drizzle with melted butter. Season with salt and pepper or a squeeze of fresh lemon juice.
- Serve hot.

Amounts of fresh herbs for infusion
basil: 10 leaves; Thai basil: 6 leaves; mint: 8 leaves; tarragon: 1 stem; oregano: 4 stems; thyme: 2 sprigs; lemon grass: 1 stem, coarsely chopped

Chef's notes: Steamed zucchini tastes even better with flavoured butter rather than plain. See the notes on page 62 for making flavoured butters. • Baby zucchini can also be skewered and grilled on the barbecue. Lightly oil and season the zucchini, place them on skewers, and cook 6–8 minutes on a medium-hot part of the grill, turning occasionally. Don't overcook them!

Oven-Baked Zucchini

Makes 4 servings

Nutritional data per 175-g serving: Calories 160; fat 15 g;
sodium 750 mg; carbohydrates 5 g; dietary fibre 2 g.

4	small zucchini	4
2	large eggs	2
2 cups	fresh white bread crumbs	500 mL
⅓ cup	melted butter	85 mL
	salt and pepper, to taste	

- Preheat oven to 400°F (200°C).
- Cut zucchini into ½-inch (1-cm) slices. Cut each slice into bite-size pieces.
- In a medium bowl, beat the eggs well with a whisk.
- In a large bowl, mix together the bread crumbs and melted butter. Season with salt and pepper.
- Dip the zucchini pieces in the beaten egg; drain lightly. Thoroughly coat the dipped zucchini in the bread-crumb mixture. Place the pieces on a baking sheet. Do not stack the pieces or they will stick together.
- Bake breaded zucchini on the top shelf in the oven, turning once during baking. Cook until the pieces are crisp, about 8–10 minutes.
- Serve immediately.

Chef's notes: I have also made this recipe on a piece of tinfoil on the barbecue. Turn the pieces once while cooking. • For extra flavour, use seasoned bread crumbs.

Stuffed Zucchini Boats

Makes 6 servings

Nutritional data per 200-g serving: Calories 140; fat 4 g;
sodium 380 mg; carbohydrates 23 g; dietary fibre 4 g.

1 tbsp.	golden raisins	15 mL
pinch	saffron	pinch
1 tbsp.	hot water	15 mL
6	small zucchini	6
	vegetable oil	
	salt and pepper, to taste	
1 cup	cooked arborio rice	250 mL
3 tbsp.	finely grated Parmesan cheese	45 mL
1 tbsp.	butter	15 mL
2 tbsp.	chopped fresh parsley	30 mL
4 or 5 pieces	sun-dried tomatoes	4 or 5 pieces

- Soak the raisins in a small dish of warm water for 10–15 minutes; set aside.
- In a small dish, soak the saffron strands in the hot water; set aside.
- Preheat oven to 350°F (175°C).
- Trim the ends of the zucchini; split the zucchini in half lengthwise. With a melon-baller or kitchen spoon, scoop out the seeds and core from the zucchini halves. Using a vegetable peeler, remove a strip from the base of each zucchini half so that it will sit flat without tipping over. Score the base of each piece lightly with cross cuts. Brush the inside of each piece with oil and season lightly.
- Measure the cooked rice into a medium bowl. Add the saffron strands with the soaking water; mix well.
- Add the Parmesan cheese, butter, parsley, and sun-dried tomatoes. Drain the raisins and add to the mixture. Season with salt and pepper.
- Fill the zucchini boats with the rice mixture. Place boats on a baking sheet and bake 8–10 minutes. Serve immediately; do not overbake.

Chef's notes: You can also grill the zucchini boats on the barbecue over medium heat.

Sweet and Sour Zucchini

Makes 4 servings

*Nutritional data per 240-g serving: Calories 140; fat 3 g;
sodium 490 mg; carbohydrates 23 g; dietary fibre 3 g.*

3	small zucchini, cut in medium dice	3
3 tbsp.	cornstarch	45 mL
2 tbsp.	light soy sauce	30 mL
1 tbsp.	sweet chili sauce	15 mL
1 tbsp.	teriyaki sauce	15 mL
2 tbsp.	brown sugar	30 mL
$\frac{1}{4}$ cup	apple-cider vinegar	65 mL
2 tsp.	grated ginger root	10 mL
12-oz. can	pineapple chunks and juice	340-mL can
$\frac{1}{2}$	large green pepper, thinly sliced	$\frac{1}{2}$
$\frac{1}{2}$	large red pepper, thinly sliced	$\frac{1}{2}$
6 oz.	firm tofu, diced	180 g
4	green onions, chopped	4

- Preheat oven to 350°F (175°C).
- In an ovenproof casserole dish with a lid, mix together the zucchini and cornstarch. Stir in the soy sauce, chili sauce, teriyaki sauce, brown sugar, and vinegar.
- Add the ginger root, pineapple and juice, and pepper slices; mix all ingredients well. Cover and bake for 20 minutes. Remove from oven and stir; cover again and bake for an additional 15 minutes. Remove from oven.
- Add the diced tofu, cover and return to the oven for another 10 minutes.
- Serve over rice, garnished with chopped green onions

Chef's notes: This dish is excellent served with grilled chicken or pork.

Marinated Vegetable Noodles

Makes 4 servings

Nutritional data per 230-g serving: Calories 60; fat 0 g;
sodium 1920 mg; carbohydrates 14 g; dietary fibre 2 g.

3	small zucchini	3
1	long English cucumber	1
½ cup	rice-wine vinegar	125 mL
1 tbsp.	sea salt	15 mL
2 cups	chunky-style salsa	500 mL

- Using a vegetable peeler or mandolin, slice the zucchini and cucumber into thin strips.
- Lay the strips out and cut with a sharp knife into thin strands, about the same size as fettuccini pasta. Put the strands into a bowl, and add the vinegar and salt. Toss the mixture together and let stand 35–40 minutes.
- Drain the strands in a colander and rinse under cold water. Drain well; the strands should be soft and palpable.
- Divide strands into serving bowls and top with salsa.
- Serve with fresh bread.

Chef's notes: Leave the peel on the vegetables when you make this dish. The extra colour looks great.

Did you know...?

To extend your growing season, seed a few zucchini plants a week or two before the average date of the last spring frost in your area. The risk of loss is small, and if the plants do freeze, the seed is fairly inexpensive so it's well worth the chance. But remember that zucchini does not like cold, wet soil, so seed early only if the weather has been favourable.

Marinated Zucchini

Makes 4 servings

Nutritional data per 175-g serving: Calories 160; fat 15 g; sodium 1740 mg; carbohydrates 7 g; dietary fibre 3 g.

4	small zucchini	4
¼ cup	olive oil	65 mL
3	garlic cloves, crushed	3
10	fresh basil leaves, chopped	10
1 tbsp.	sea salt	15 mL
1 tbsp.	ground black pepper	15 mL
2 tbsp.	balsamic vinegar	30 mL

- Slice zucchini lengthwise into ¼-inch (0.5-cm) slices.
- Heat oil in a wok or deep frying pan over medium-high heat. The oil should be just smoking.
- Cook the zucchini slices, a few at a time, until they are golden-brown, about 2 minutes on each side. Remove the cooked strips and drain on paper towel.
- In a medium bowl, combine the garlic, basil, salt, and pepper; mix well.
- Place a few of the cooked zucchini strips on the bottom of a glass 9-inch (23-cm) pie plate. With a spoon, spread some of the herb mixture over the zucchini. Drizzle with balsamic vinegar. Repeat with another layer of zucchini strips, until all the strips, herb mixture, and vinegar are used.
- Cover with plastic wrap and refrigerate 4 hours.
- Serve on fresh salad greens or on grilled bread.

Baby Zucchini with Peas and Corn

Makes 4–6 servings

Nutritional data per 215-g serving: Calories 110; fat 4 g; sodium 550 mg; carbohydrates 15 g; dietary fibre 4 g.

2 tbsp.	vegetable oil	30 mL
4	small garlic cloves, crushed	4
2	celery stalks, finely diced	2
1	medium red onion, finely diced	1
½ tsp.	cumin	2.5 mL
½ tsp.	turmeric	2.5 mL
24	baby zucchini	24
2 cups	canned tomatoes, chopped, with juice	500 mL
½ cup	frozen peas, thawed	125 mL
½ cup	frozen kernel corn, thawed	125 mL
	salt and pepper, to taste	

- In a large skillet, heat the oil over medium heat. Add the garlic, celery, and onion; cook for 2-3 minutes, until the vegetables are soft. Stir in the cumin and turmeric; cook for 1 minute.
- Add the zucchini; cook for 5 minutes. Add the chopped tomatoes, peas, and corn; season with salt and pepper. Reduce heat to medium-low. Cook for 10–12 minutes, until the zucchini are just tender.
- Serve with basmati rice, brown rice, or couscous.

Chef's notes: For a variation, use medium-hot chunky salsa in place of the canned tomatoes. • If the baby zucchini are too big, cut them in half on the bias.

Sautéed Onions with Zucchini

Makes 4 servings

Nutritional data per 190-g serving: Calories 350; fat 32 g; sodium 5 mg; carbohydrates 7 g; dietary fibre 2 g.

½ cup	vegetable oil	125 mL
1	large white onion, sliced	1
1	large red onion, sliced	1
1 cup	dry white wine	250 mL
1 tbsp.	chopped fresh thyme	15 mL
1 tbsp.	vegetable oil	15 mL
4	small zucchini, cut into rounds	4
	salt and pepper, to taste	
2 tbsp.	chopped fresh parsley	30 mL

- In a large skillet, heat ½ cup (125 mL) vegetable oil over medium-high heat. Add the sliced onions and sauté, stirring occasionally, for 3-4 minutes, until the onions begin to colour and soften.
- Add the wine and cook for another 7–8 minutes, until onions are soft. Add the chopped thyme; cook for 1 minute, then remove from heat. Transfer mixture to a bowl and keep warm.
- Add the remaining 1 tbsp. (15 mL) oil to the sauté pan. Over medium-high heat, toss the zucchini rounds until they are just cooked and still crisp. Season with salt and pepper.
- Make a small bed of onions on a plate and top with sautéed zucchini. Sprinkle with parsley.
- Serve warm with fresh bread.

Chef's notes: If fresh thyme is not available, use 1 tsp. (5 mL) dried thyme.

Stuffed Zucchini

Makes 4 servings

*Nutritional data per 100-g serving: Calories 80; fat 4 g;
sodium 250 mg; carbohydrates 8 g; dietary fibre 1 g.*

2	medium zucchini	2
	boiling salted water, for blanching	
2 tbsp.	vegetable oil	30 mL
1	medium onion, firely diced	1
2	medium celery stalks, finely diced	2
3 tbsp.	chopped fresh parsley	45 mL
1 tsp.	chopped fresh thyme	5 mL
2 tbsp.	tomato paste	30 mL
½ cup	fresh white bread crumbs	125 mL
1 cup	chicken stock	250 mL
1	large egg	1
	salt and pepper, to taste	

- Preheat oven to 350°F (175°C).
- Cut each zucchini into 2 equal pieces. With a melon-baller or kitchen spoon, hollow out the centre of each piece of zucchini.
- Blanch zucchini pieces in boiling salted water for 1 minute. Rinse zucchini under cold running water and drain well; set aside.
- Heat the oil in a medium skillet. Add the onions and celery; cook for 4 minutes, stirring constantly. Add the parsley and thyme; cook for 1 minute.
- Stir in the tomato paste and add the bread crumbs; mix well. Remove from heat.
- Cool mixture for 5 minutes. Add the beaten egg and ¼ of the chicken broth to moisten the mix. Season mix with salt and pepper.
- Fill a piping bag with the bread-crumb mix and fill the cavities of the blanched zucchini.
- Place the stuffed zucchini halves in a shallow baking dish. Add the remaining chicken broth and cover the dish with aluminum foil.
- Bake covered dish for 10–12 minutes, until zucchini is cooked but still firm.
- Cool for 5 minutes, slice, and serve.

Chef's notes: The filling and zucchini pieces can be made in advance, then combined and baked immediately prior to serving.

Zucchini Stuffed with Pine Nuts

Makes 8–10 servings

Nutritional data per 220-g serving: Calories 450; fat 22 g; sodium 520 mg; carbohydrates 45 g; dietary fibre 5 g.

2½ lbs.	whole zucchini	1.2 kg
2 tbsp.	vegetable oil	30 mL
1	large onion, diced	1
1 lb.	lean ground pork	500 g
4	fresh sage leaves, chopped	4
2 tsp.	chopped fresh thyme	10 mL
3 tbsp.	chopped fresh parsley	45 mL
	salt and pepper, to taste	
2 cups	fresh white bread crumbs	500 g
1	Granny Smith apple, peeled, cored, and diced	1
¾ cup	pine nuts	195 mL

- Cut the stalk off the zucchini and reserve the cut end. With a melon-baller or kitchen spoon, scoop out the seeds and make a cavity for the stuffing.
- Heat the oil in a large skillet over medium heat. Add the onion and cook 4–5 minutes, until soft. Add the ground pork and cook well, about 5–6 minutes. Add the chopped herbs; season with salt and pepper. Remove pan from heat.
- Stir in the bread crumbs, apple, and pine nuts. Mix the dressing well and allow to cool.
- Preheat oven to 400°F (200°C).
- Stuff the zucchini with the cooled dressing. Replace the cut end and secure with wooden skewers.
- Wrap the zucchini in aluminum foil (shiny side in) and place in a large baking dish. Bake for about 1 hour. Test for doneness with skewer; the zucchini will feel tender when tested.
- Slice and serve.

Chef's notes: The skin on the large zucchini will be tough. You can peel the zucchini, but I find that leaving the skin on adds a better flavour to the flesh and helps the zucchini hold its shape during baking.

Barley Risotto with Zucchini

Makes 4–6 servings

*Nutritional data per 160-g serving: Calories 360; fat 11 g;
sodium 580 mg; carbohydrates 54 g; dietary fibre 12 g.*

2 tbsp.	butter	30 mL
1	medium onion, finely chopped	1
5 cups	chicken stock	1.25 L
2 stems	lemongrass, finely chopped	2 stems
2 cups	barley	500 mL
1 cup	grated zucchini	250 mL
½ cup	grated Parmesan cheese	125 mL
	salt and pepper, to taste	
1 tbsp.	butter	15 mL

- In a heavy medium saucepan melt 2 tbsp. (30 mL) butter over medium heat. Add the chopped onion and cook for 3–4 minutes, stirring constantly. Remove pan from heat.
- In a medium saucepan, heat the chicken stock with the lemongrass. Bring to a boil, reduce heat, and simmer gently for 8–10 minutes. Remove from heat and strain the stock to remove the lemongrass pieces.
- Return the saucepan containing the onions to the stove and warm over medium heat. Add the barley and stir until the grains are coated.
- Add a small amount of the stock to the onion-barley mixture and stir until the liquid is absorbed. Repeat this procedure until the barley is soft but not overcooked (about 20 minutes). Discard any remaining stock.
- Add the Parmesan cheese and the remaining butter; stir until fully incorporated.
- Remove from heat and season. Serve immediately.

Polenta with Zucchini

Makes 6–8 servings

Nutritional data per 320-g serving: Calories 330; fat 10 g; sodium 10 mg; carbohydrates 53 g; dietary fibre 5 g.

6 cups	water	1.5 L
2 tsp.	salt	30 mL
1 lb.	yellow cornmeal	454 g
1 cup	grated zucchini	250 mL
¼ cup	vegetable oil	65 mL

- In a heavy-bottomed saucepan, bring the water to a boil; add salt.
- Stir the cornmeal and zucchini into the boiling water. Reduce heat to medium. Stir the mixture with a wooden spoon until it leaves the sides of the saucepan, about 5 minutes.
- Spread the mixture in an even layer on a 9-inch (23-cm) pie plate. Cover and refrigerate 4 hours.
- Cut the chilled polenta into wedges or attractive shapes.
- Heat the vegetable oil over medium heat in a large sauté pan. Sauté the polenta pieces for 3 minutes on each side.
- Serve hot.

Chef's notes: For extra flavour, stir in 1 tbsp. (15 mL) of fresh herbs (such as thyme, oregano, parsley, basil, and chives) with the cornmeal and zucchini. You can also add 3 tbsp. (45 mL) chopped sun-dried tomatoes. • For a delicious variation, top the fried polenta with your favourite grated or sliced cheese and broil until the cheese is melted.

Did you know...?

Zucchini bears both male and female flowers on the same plant. The male flowers do not produce fruit but supply the pollen that fertilizes the female flowers. The pollen is sticky, so wind pollination does not occur; instead, the pollen must be transferred by insects in order for the fruit to develop. Bees are the most common insects to transfer pollen, and farmers who grow squashes commercially often install hives of bees in their fields to ensure that pollination takes place.

Zucchini Fried Rice

Makes 6 servings

Nutritional data per 165-g serving: Calories 200; fat 7 g; sodium 340 mg; carbohydrates 32 g; dietary fibre 2 g.

1 tsp.	sesame oil	5 mL
2 tbsp.	vegetable oil	30 mL
1	medium carrot, finely diced	1
3	stalks of celery, chopped	3
6	mushrooms, chopped	6
6	green onions, chopped	6
2	small zucchini, finely diced	2
2 cups	cooked basmati rice	500 mL
1 tbsp.	sesame seeds	15 mL
1 tsp.	5-spice powder	5 mL
2 tbsp.	light soy sauce	30 mL
	sesame seeds for garnish	

- In a wok or skillet, heat the oils over medium heat. Add carrot and celery. Cook for 3-4 minutes, stirring frequently, until the vegetables are tender.
- Add the mushrooms, green onions, and zucchini. Cook for 2-3 minutes, stirring occasionally.
- Gently stir in the cooked rice. Season with 5-spice powder and add soy sauce.
- Serve hot, sprinkled with sesame seeds.

Chef's notes: Stir this mixture with chopsticks to keep it light and prevent it from becoming too sticky.

Hash Browns Southwestern Style

Makes 12–14 cakes

*Nutritional data per 120-g serving: Calories 50; fat 2 g;
sodium 360 mg; carbohydrates 5 g; dietary fibre 2 g.*

4 cups	grated zucchini	1 L
1 tbsp.	salt	15 mL
2	large eggs, beaten	2
½ cup	grated Parmesan cheese	125 mL
2	garlic cloves, minced	2
1 tbsp.	chili powder	15 mL
½ cup	chopped green onion	125 mL
½ cup	instant potato flakes	125 mL
	salt and pepper, to taste	
3 tbsp.	vegetable oil	45 mL

• In a large bowl, mix the grated zucchini with salt. Let stand at room temperature for 15 minutes. Strain the mixture through a single layer of cheesecloth to remove excess liquid, then return the strained zucchini to the bowl.

• Mix in the beaten eggs, Parmesan cheese, garlic, chili powder, green onion, potato flakes, salt, and pepper. Form the mixture into small, flattened cakes.

• In a 12-inch (30-cm) skillet, heat oil over medium heat.

• Cook the cakes on both sides for about 5 minutes per side. Add more oil to the pan if necessary.

Chef's notes: Serve with salsa or sour cream. • For an extra treat, sprinkle grated cheese on the cooked patties and melt under the broiler.

Zucchini Skillet Pancakes

Makes 6–8 servings

Nutritional data per 170-g serving: Calories 200; fat 8 g;
sodium 560 mg; carbohydrates 25 g; dietary fibre 2 g.

3 cups	grated zucchini	750 mL
1 tbsp.	grated lemon zest	15 mL
1 tsp.	salt	5 mL
½ cup	grated Parmesan cheese	125 mL
2 tbsp.	chopped fresh parsley	30 mL
2 tbsp.	chopped fresh basil leaves	30 mL
1 tsp.	freshly ground black pepper	5 mL
1 cup	instant potato flakes	250 mL
¾ to 1 cup	all-purpose flour	190 to 250 mL
2 tbsp.	extra-virgin olive oil	30 mL

- Preheat oven to 350°F (190°C).
- In a large bowl, combine the zucchini, lemon zest, and salt. Let the mixture stand for 10 minutes to soften the zucchini.
- Add the Parmesan cheese, parsley, basil, and pepper. Mix well. Stir in the potato flakes and flour.
- Heat the olive oil in a 9-inch (23-cm) cast-iron skillet over medium-high heat.
- Carefully transfer the mixture into the skillet and shape into a flat pancake. Reduce heat to medium and cook the pancake for 3 minutes to form a crust on the base.
- Using a spatula, loosen the pancake in the pan. Remove from heat and place the skillet in the oven. Bake for 20 minutes.
- Remove the skillet from the oven and allow to cool for 5 minutes. Invert the pancake on a cutting board and cut into wedges. Serve immediately.

Quick Zucchini Cakes

Makes 8 patties

Nutritional data per 90-g serving: Calories 115; fat 5 g; sodium 409 mg; carbohydrates 14 g; dietary fibre 2 g.

2 cups	grated zucchini	500 mL
1	large egg, beaten	1
2 tbsp.	diced yellow onion	2 tbsp.
½ cup	fresh white bread crumbs	125 mL
2 tbsp.	chopped parsley	30 mL
	pinch of nutmeg	
	salt and pepper, to taste	
2 tbsp.	olive oil	30 mL

• In a large bowl, combine all ingredients except the olive oil. Mix well and form into 8 patties.

• In a 10-inch (25-cm) skillet, heat the oil and fry the patties for 5 minutes per side or until golden-brown. Remove patties from skillet and place on paper towel to drain excess oil.

• Serve hot.

Chef's notes: Patties can be topped with grated cheddar or mozzarella cheese and broiled for 2 minutes. • Serve patties with salsa or relish (see pages 135–36 for some recipe suggestions).

Entrées

Zucchini Care and Nurture

Although zucchini is a vigorous, prolific plant, it is susceptible to a few diseases and pests.

Blossom-end rot: *When the soil moisture fluctuates rapidly (for example, a period of drought followed by a downpour), zucchini can suffer from blossom-end rot. The fruits collapse and rot from the tip. Blossom-end rot is brought on by a lack of calcium. When the plant lacks moisture, the calcium cannot be transported to the blossom end of the fruit. Water regularly and add fertilizer around the base of the plant to help prevent this condition.*

Cucumber mosaic virus: *When infected with the cucumber mosaic virus, zucchini will suffer from stunted growth and mottled foliage. The virus is primarily transmitted to zucchini by aphids, but it may also be transmitted by the spotted cucumber beetle. To inhibit spread of this virus, keep a tight rein on weeds and insect pests. Avoid touching other plants if you've handled infected zucchini plants: you can spread the virus with your hands. Zucchini can also be infected by squash mosaic virus and zucchini yellow mosaic virus, with similar results.*

Salmon with Zucchini

Makes 4 servings

*Nutritional data per 220-g serving: Calories 180; fat 7 g;
sodium 270 mg; carbohydrates 5 g; dietary fibre 2 g.*

4 4-oz.	salmon fillets	4 120-g
2 tsp.	dried tarragon	10 mL
2 tsp.	lemon pepper	10 mL
1 tbsp.	lime juice	15 mL
2	Roma tomatoes, diced	2
2	small zucchini, diced	2

- Place salmon fillets on a microwave-safe dish or dinner plate. Sprinkle with tarragon and lemon pepper. Pour the lime juice around the fillets, then sprinkle the zucchini and tomatoes over the fillets.
- Cover the dish with plastic wrap or microwave-safe cover. Cook on high for 4 minutes.
- Check the fish for doneness by separating the flesh with a fork. It will flake easily when the fish is cooked. If necessary, cook for another 2 minutes.
- Serve immediately.

Chef's notes: This recipe takes just a few minutes to prepare. I like to serve it with steamed rice. It's great with the mint chutney on page 138. • Use any leftover fish as a sandwich filling the next day. Just mix the leftovers, vegetables and all, with a spoonful of mayonnaise.

Sea Bass with Lemongrass and Zucchini

Makes 4 servings

Nutritional data per 120-g serving: Calories 170; fat 11 g;
sodium 55 mg; carbohydrates 3 g; dietary fibre 1

4 4-oz.	sea bass fillets	4 120-g
2 tbsp.	lime juice	30 mL
2	small zucchini, sliced into rounds	2
2 stems	lemongrass, finely chopped	2 stems
⅓ cup	coconut cream	85 mL

- Preheat oven 350°F (175°C).
- Place the sea bass fillets in a shallow baking dish or glass pie plate and rub with lime juice. Let stand for 10 minutes.
- Place zucchini in steamer basket or perforated steamer.
- Chop the tender part of the lemongrass stem and place in the steamer with the zucchini rounds. Chop the tops of the lemongrass and add to the water in the steamer pot to infuse the flavour into the zucchini.
- Steam zucchini 8–10 minutes, until tender. Drain any excess liquid. Purée the zucchini in blender. Add the coconut cream and blend in quickly.
- Pour the sauce around fish in the baking dish, cover with aluminum foil, and bake on middle rack for 15–20 minutes.
- Serve immediately.

Chef's notes: For an elegant presentation, garnish this dish with lime wedges and fresh cilantro leaves. • Offer hot chili sauce at the table with this recipe.
- This dish is excellent with coconut sticky rice.

Zucchini-Rolled Sole

Makes 4 servings

*Nutritional data per 120-g serving: Calories 90; fat 1 g;
sodium 35 mg; carbohydrates 2 g; dietary fibre 0 g.*

4 slices	grilled zucchini	4 slices
4 3-oz	boneless, skinless sole fillets	4 90-g
	lemon or lime juice	
1 tbsp.	fresh chopped parsley	15 mL
1 tbsp.	chopped chives	15 mL
	lemon pepper for seasoning	

- Grill 4 zucchini strips, using the method on page 25.
- Set the grilled zucchini strips on a flat surface; season with lemon pepper.
- Place the sole fillets on top of the zucchini strips, with the whitest part of the meat facing the zucchini. Squeeze a few drops of lemon or lime juice on each fish fillet. Sprinkle with parsley and chives.
- Roll the sole and zucchini together in a fairly tight roll; secure the rolled piece with a toothpick.
- Grease a 9-inch (23-cm) glass pie plate or oven-proof casserole dish and place the rolls in it, flat side down.
- Squeeze a few more drops of lemon or lime juice over the fish; cover dish lightly with aluminum foil. Cook for 15–20 minutes at 350°F (175°C). Serve hot.

Chef's notes: For extra flavour, spread a simple bread-crumb dressing on the fish fillets before rolling them. • Serve this dish with seasoned butter or Hollandaise sauce. • This recipe can be made in the microwave oven. Proceed as directed, but cover with plastic wrap instead of aluminum foil. Cook in the microwave for 4–5 minutes.

Crab Cakes

Makes 4 servings

Nutritional data per 300-g serving: Calories 510; fat 14 g; sodium 680 mg; carbohydrates 70 g; dietary fibre 6 g.

4 cups	grated zucchini	1 L
1 tbsp.	salt	15 mL
7.5 oz.	canned crab meat, drained	213 g
3 cups	fresh white bread crumbs	750 mL
2	large eggs	2
2 tbsp.	mayonnaise	30 mL
1 tbsp.	tomato ketchup	15 mL
1 tbsp.	lemon juice	15 mL
2 tbsp.	chopped parsley	30 mL
2 tsp.	lemon pepper	10 mL
	vegetable oil for frying	
	lemon or lime wedges for garnish	

- Mix the zucchini and salt in a medium bowl and let sit for 30 minutes. Squeeze the zucchini through a single layer of cheesecloth until it is quite dry.
- In a large bowl, mix the drained zucchini with the rest of the ingredients. Form the mixture into patties.
- In a skillet, fry patties in a small amount of oil over medium heat until brown on both sides.
- Serve patties hot with lime or lemon wedges.

Did you know...?

Contrary to expectation, domestic zucchini production satisfies only about 25% of Canada's demand for the vegetable, probably due to our brief growing season and the short storage time for fresh young zucchini. You really never can have enough!

Baked Salmon with Zucchini

Makes 4 servings

Nutritional data per 120-g serving: Calories 200; fat 3 g; sodium 90 mg; carbohydrates 11 g; dietary fibre 0 g.

4 4-oz	boneless, skinless salmon fillets	4 120-g
1 tbsp.	vegetable oil	15 mL
1 tbsp.	lime juice	15 mL
1 tsp.	grated ginger root	5 mL
1 tbsp.	sweet chili sauce	15 mL
1 tsp.	finely chopped lemongrass	5 mL
1	small zucchini, cut in thin slices	1
1 tbsp.	rice wine vinegar	15 mL
1 tsp.	5-spice powder	5 mL
	lime or lemon wedges, for garnish	

- Preheat oven to 350°F (175°C).
- Place the salmon fillets in a large bowl with the vegetable oil, lime juice, grated ginger, chili sauce, and lemongrass. Marinate for 10 minutes.
- In a separate bowl, mix the zucchini slices, rice wine vinegar and 5-spice powder; marinate for 5 minutes.
- Remove salmon from marinade. With a small sharp knife, make an incision in each fillet to form a small pocket.
- Stuff each pocket with some of the zucchini slices. Place the salmon fillets in a shallow oven-proof dish.
- Bake the fish in the oven on the top rack for 12–15 minutes, until the fish flakes easily with a fork.
- Serve with fresh lime or lemon wedges.

Chef's notes: Coconut rice makes a great side dish for this recipe.

Baked Meatloaf

Makes 6 servings

Nutritional data per 230-g serving: Calories 350; fat 18 g; sodium 920 mg; carbohydrates 20 g; dietary fibre 2 g.

1½ lbs.	lean ground beef	675 g
1 cup	fresh white bread crumbs	250 mL
2	large eggs	2
1	medium onion, finely chopped	1
1 cup	grated zucchini	250 mL
1 cup	tomato sauce	250 mL
2 tsp.	chopped fresh thyme	10 mL
2 tbsp.	grated Parmesan cheese	30 mL
2 tbsp.	Worcestershire sauce	30 mL
	salt and pepper, to taste	

- Preheat oven to 350°F (175°C).
- In a large bowl, combine all ingredients; mix well.
- Place the mixture in a 8x4-inch (20x10-cm) loaf pan and bake for 1 hour. Test for doneness with a meat thermometer; the internal temperature should read 165°F (75°C).
- Serve immediately.

Chef's notes: This mixture can also be used for making meatballs. Form the mixture into bite-size rounds. Bake the meatballs for 10 minutes at 350°F (175°C). Serve with your favourite sauce or on toothpicks as an appetizer.

Zucchini Frittata

Makes 4–6 servings

Nutritional data per 145-g serving: Calories 100; fat 7 g; sodium 100 mg; carbohydrates 5 g, dietary fibre 1 g.

1 tbsp.	extra-virgin olive oil	15 mL
3	garlic cloves, chopped	3
1	small yellow onion, finely diced	1
3 cups	grated zucchini	750 mL
4	large eggs	4
1/3 cup	cereal cream	85 mL
1 tsp.	chopped fresh thyme	5 mL
1 tsp.	chopped fresh basil	5 mL
1 tsp.	chopped fresh oregano	5 mL
	salt and pepper, to taste	
12	black olives, drained and pitted	12
3	small Roma tomatoes, thinly sliced	3

- Preheat oven to 350°F (175°C).
- Heat the oil in a 10-inch (25-cm) cast-iron skillet over medium heat. Add garlic and cook for 1 minute, stirring constantly. Do not let the garlic burn. Add onion and cook for 3 minutes.
- Add the zucchini and sauté, stirring constantly, about 4–5 minutes. When zucchini is cooked, drain off any excess liquid.
- In a medium bowl, mix eggs, cream, herbs, salt, and pepper. Add the black olives.
- Add the egg mixture to the skillet and cook for 1 minute to set.
- Remove skillet from stove and place in the oven. Bake frittata for 5–6 minutes. Remove skillet from oven and layer frittata with sliced tomatoes. Return skillet to oven and bake frittata another 7–8 minutes, or until eggs are completely cooked.

Zucchini Soufflés

Makes 10 individual soufflés

*Nutritional data per 70-g serving: Calories 80; fat 6 g;
sodium 300 mg; carbohydrates 4 g; dietary fibre 1 g.*

1½ cups	grated zucchini	375 mL
4 tbsp.	butter	60 mL
4 tbsp.	all-purpose flour	60 mL
⅓ cup	milk	85 mL
2 tbsp.	chopped chives	30 mL
2 tbsp.	chopped parsley	30 mL
	pinch of nutmeg	
	salt and pepper, to taste	
3	eggs, at room temperature	3

- Lightly grease muffin tins.
- Steam the zucchini for 6–8 minutes until very tender. Drain and cool.
- Purée the cooked zucchini in a food processor with a blade attachment. Strain the purée through a single layer of cheesecloth and squeeze out as much liquid as possible.
- In a heavy-bottomed medium saucepan, melt the butter. Stir in the flour and cook for 1 minute. Add the milk and stir to form a smooth paste.
- Add the chives, parsley, nutmeg, salt, pepper, and the zucchini purée.
- Separate the egg yolks and whites. Add the egg yolks to the zucchini mixture.
- Beat the egg whites in a medium bowl until they form stiff peaks. Fold the beaten egg whites into the zucchini mixture with a wooden spoon or rubber spatula; do this in three small batches to prevent overmixing. (The egg whites may not be completely incorporated.)
- Spoon about ½ cup (125 mL) of the mixture into each muffin cup. Do not overfill cups.
- Bake at 375°F (190°C) for 8–10 minutes, or until the tops are brown. Let the finished soufflés stand in the tins for about 5 minutes before serving, so they will be easier to remove.

Chef's notes: Try adding chopped fresh thyme, oregano, or basil leaves. • Top with Parmesan, cheddar, or blue cheese.

Ratatouille

Makes 4–6 servings

Nutritional data per 130-g serving: Calories 90; fat 6 g; sodium 40 mg; carbohydrates 8 g; dietary fibre 1 g.

1	small red pepper, diced	1
1	small green pepper, diced	1
3	Roma tomatoes, chopped	3
3	small zucchini, diced	3
1	eggplant, diced	1
2 tbsp.	tomato paste	30 mL
⅓ cup	dry white wine	85 mL
2 tsp.	granulated sugar	10 mL
1 tbsp.	chopped fresh thyme	15 mL
⅓ cup	olive oil	85 mL
4	garlic cloves, chopped	4
1	medium yellow onion	1
1	bay leaf	1
	salt and pepper, to taste	

- Chop all the vegetables and set aside in separate bowls.
- In a small bowl, mix the tomato paste, white wine, sugar, and thyme; set aside.
- Heat the olive oil in a 12-inch (30-cm) skillet over medium heat. Add the garlic and cook for 1 minute, stirring constantly. Add the onion and cook for 4–5 minutes, until tender. Add the red and green peppers; cook for 3–4 minutes.
- Add the eggplant and zucchini; mix all the vegetables well. Cook for 3 minutes. Add the tomato-paste mixture and cook for 2 minutes. Add the chopped tomatoes. Stir gently and cook for 2 minutes.
- Season to taste with salt and pepper and serve immediately.

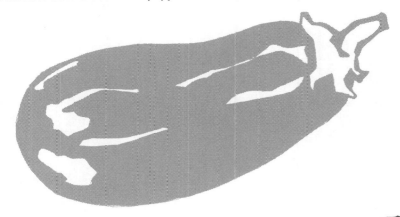

Zucchini Curry with Beans and Corn

Makes 4–6 servings

Nutritional data per 160-g serving: Calories 140; fat 2 g;
sodium 525 mg; carbohydrates 25 g; dietary fibre 5 g.

2	small zucchini, diced	2
12-oz. can	kernel corn, drained	340-mL can
2 cups	garbanzo beans, drained	500 mL
1 tbsp.	prepared curry paste	15 mL
1 tsp.	salt	5 mL
4	whole green onions, chopped	4

- In medium bowl, mix together the diced zucchini, corn, garbanzo beans, curry paste, salt, and green onions.
- Place the ingredients into a microwave container and cover loosely with a lid to allow for venting.
- Cook on high power for 5 minutes. Check after 4 minutes for doneness and temperature.
- Serve with pita bread or over brown rice.

Did you know...?

According to the *Guinness Book of World Records*,
the largest zucchini ever grown weighed 36 pounds,
3 ounces and measured 29.5 inches. It was grown in Montreal.

Sautéed Zucchini with Herb and Tomato Salsa

Makes 4 servings

Nutritional data per 210-g serving: Calories 120; fat 8 g; sodium 320 mg; carbohydrates 13 g; dietary fibre 7 g

3 tbsp.	olive oil	45 mL
1	medium red onion, finely chopped	1
4	small zucchini, finely diced	4
1½ cups	medium-hot tomato salsa	375 mL
10	fresh basil leaves, chopped	10
3 tbsp.	chopped fresh parsley	45 mL
2 tsp.	granulated sugar	10 mL

- In a large skillet, heat the olive oil over medium heat. Add the onion and cook for 4–5 minutes, until soft.
- Add the diced zucchini and sauté until the zucchini is tender, about 4-5 minutes. Reduce any excess liquid.
- Stir in the salsa, basil, and parsley. Cook until the mixture is quite dry. Add the sugar and cook for 1 minute longer. Remove from heat.
- Serve warm over rice or egg noodles.

Chef's notes: This dish makes a good topping for grilled bread slices. • Stir a container of sour cream into this recipe and serve warm or chilled for a tasty dip.

Vegetable Stew

Makes 4 servings

Nutritional data per 350-g serving: Calories 290; fat 15 g; sodium 1260 mg; carbohydrates 29 g; dietary fibre 4 g.

¼ cup	olive oil	65 mL
4	shallots, quartered	4
6	green onions, chopped into short lengths	6
8	field mushrooms, stemmed, quartered	8
12	baby zucchini	12
1 cup	frozen peas, thawed	250 mL
10 oz.	canned whole baby corn, drained	375 mL
2 tbsp.	chopped fresh basil	30 mL
2 tbsp.	chopped fresh chives	30 mL
2 tbsp.	chopped fresh parsley	30 mL
2 cups	tomato juice	500 mL
	salt and pepper, to taste	

- Heat the olive oil in a large sauté pan over medium-high heat. Add the shallots, green onions, mushrooms, and baby zucchini. Toss the vegetables in the pan for 2 minutes, until they begin to soften. Add the peas and corn; cook for 2 minutes.
- Add the chopped herbs; mix well. Add the tomato juice. Reduce heat to medium and cook for 3–4 minutes. Season to taste.
- Serve hot over pasta or rice.

Baby Zucchini Curry

Makes 4–6 servings

Nutritional data per 300-g serving: Calories 140; fat 2 g; sodium 870 mg; carbohydrates 27 g; dietary fibre 5 g.

2 tbsp.	vegetable oil	30 mL
3	garlic cloves, crushed	3
1	medium onion, finely diced	1
2	celery stalks, finely diced	2
1 tbsp.	curry paste	15 mL
2 tbsp.	tomato paste	30 mL
2	medium tomatoes, finely diced	2
24	baby zucchini	24
15 oz.	canned chick peas, drained	375 mL
1 cup	chicken broth	250 mL
	salt and pepper, to taste	

- Heat the oil in a large skillet over medium heat. Add the garlic, onion, and celery; cook 4–5 minutes. Stir in the curry paste; cook for 1 minute.
- Stir in the tomato paste. If the mixture is too thick, add some of the chicken broth.
- Add the diced tomato and the baby zucchini; season with salt and pepper. Add the chicken broth and chick peas; cook for 5–6 minutes until the zucchini are tender.
- Serve over pasta, rice, or couscous.

Chef's notes: Underripe tomatoes or even green tomatoes work well in this recipe. Add them with the sautéed onion, celery, and garlic.

Zucchini-Potato Patties

Makes 10 patties

*Nutritional data per 100-g serving: Calories 100; fat 6 g;
sodium 75 mg; carbohydrates 10 g; dietary fibre 2 g.*

1 lb.	zucchini	450 g
1 lb.	Yukon Gold potatoes	450 g
1 tbsp.	chopped chives	15 mL
1 tbsp.	Italian seasoning	15 mL
	salt and pepper, to taste	
¼ cup	extra-virgin olive oil	65 mL

• Grate the zucchini and squeeze out any excess liquid. Peel and grate the potatoes, then squeeze out any excess liquid. Mix the zucchini and potatoes in a medium bowl.

• Add the chopped chives. Season with Italian seasoning, salt, and pepper. Form mixture into 10 patties; do not allow the mixture to stand.

• Heat the olive oil in a 12-inch (30-cm) skillet over medium heat. Cook the patties for 5 minutes on each side or until golden-brown.

Chef's notes: If the mixture is too moist, add 2 tbsp. (30 mL) of instant mashed potato flakes and mix well before forming patties. • Serve patties with salsa or tomato ketchup.

Baby Zucchini with Tricolour Pasta

Makes 4–6 servings

*Nutritional data per 210-g serving: Calories 440; fat 35 g;
sodium 125 mg; carbohydrates 26 g, dietary fibre 1 g.*

3 cups	tricolour fusili pasta	750 mL
4	Roma tomatoes	4
1/4 cup	olive oil	65 mL
24 to 30	baby zucchini, sliced lengthwise	24 to 30
3	garlic cloves, chopped	3
10	large basil leaves, chopped	10
1 1/2 cups	heavy cream	375 mL
	salt and black pepper, to taste	
2 tbsp.	flat-leaf parsley, chopped	30 mL
1/3 cup	grated Parmesan cheese	85 mL

- Cook the pasta according to package directions. Set aside but keep warm.
- Blanch the tomatoes by plunging them in boiling water for 1 minute, then cooling in cold water. Remove the peel and seeds, then chop coarsely.
- Heat the oil in a large saucepan over medium-high heat. The oil must be hot. Add the sliced zucchini and cook until the zucchini begins to turn golden-brown. Add the garlic, tomatoes, and basil leaves; pour the cream over the ingredients.
- Shake the pan to mix the ingredients; season with salt and pepper. Cook for 1-2 minutes.
- Spoon sauce over the tricolour pasta, sprinkle with parsley and Parmesan cheese, and serve hot.

Bacon-Macaroni Bake

Makes 8 servings

*Nutritional data per 220-g serving: Calories 470; fat 32 g;
sodium 670 mg; carbohydrates 26 g; dietary fibre 2 g.*

4	small zucchini	4
2	large eggs	2
	salt and pepper, to taste	
2 cups	ricotta cheese	500 mL
2 cups	cooked elbow macaroni	500 mL
2 tbsp.	chopped fresh parsley	30 mL
6	green onion, chopped	6
10	slices bacon, cooked	10
1 cup	cheddar cheese, grated	250 mL

- Cut the zucchini into ¼-inch (0.5-cm) slices. Blanch the slices by cooking them in boiling salted water for 3 minutes. Drain and refresh the slices under cold water. Drain the zucchini well and set aside.
- Preheat oven to 350°F (175°C).
- In a large bowl, beat the eggs; season with salt and pepper. Stir in the ricotta cheese, cooked macaroni, and parsley.
- Layer half the blanched zucchini slices in a 9-inch (23-cm) pie plate. Layer ½ the ricotta mixture on top of the zucchini. Layer the rest of the zucchini; top with the remaining ricotta mixture. Place the bacon on top of the last layer, then sprinkle with the cheddar cheese. Bake for 40–45 minutes.
- Serve hot.

Layered Casserole

Makes 4–6 servings

Nutritional data per 390-g serving: Calories 350; fat 13 g; sodium 1180 mg; carbohydrates 40 g; dietary fibre 5 g.

6	uncooked lasagna noodles	6
2	medium zucchini	2
1	medium green pepper	1
1	medium red pepper	1
2 cups	chunky-style tomato sauce	500 mL
½ cup	grated Parmesan cheese	125 mL
10	fresh basil leaves	10
2 tbsp.	chopped fresh parsley	30 mL
½ cup	cheddar cheese, grated	125 mL
½ cup	mozzarella cheese, grated	125 mL
	ground black pepper to taste	
	oil for baking dish	

- Cook lasagna noodles according to package directions. Rinse under cold water; drain well.
- Trim the ends off zucchini and slice lengthwise into strips ¹/₈ inch (0.25 cm) thick (use a mandolin to make this step easier). Grill using the method on page 25.
- Slice peppers into strips ¼ inch (0.5 cm) thick. Grill strips 1 minute on each side; use tongs to turn.
- Preheat oven to 350°F (175°C).
- Lightly oil a 6x6-inch (15x15-cm) baking dish or casserole dish. Spread ½ cup (125 mL) of tomato sauce on the bottom of the dish.
- Cut the cooked lasagna noodles to fit the dish. Place a layer on top of the tomato sauce. Layer the grilled zucchini and peppers on top of the lasagna noodles. Sprinkle with Parmesan cheese.
- Spoon ½ cup tomato sauce over the layers. Sprinkle with parsley. Layer basil leaves over sauce; season with black pepper.
- Make another layer of lasagna noodles; layer remaining zucchini slices and pepper strips on top of the noodles. Spread layers with the remaining tomato sauce.
- Sprinkle the mozzarella and cheddar cheeses over the layers.
- Bake until the cheese is bubbling, about 35-40 minutes. Cool dish for 15 minutes before cutting and serving.

Zucchini Tuscana

Makes 10–12 servings

Nutritional data per 120-g serving: Calories 130; fat 8 g; sodium 590 mg; carbohydrates 9 g; dietary fibre 2 g.

¼ cup	extra-virgin olive oil	65 mL
1 tbsp.	chopped garlic	15 mL
1	small onion, chopped	1
2 cups	prepared chunky-style tomato sauce	500 mL
1½ lbs.	whole zucchini	680 g
2	large eggs, beaten	2
½ cup	all-purpose flour	125 mL
	salt and pepper, to taste	
1 cup	grated Parmesan cheese	250 mL
1 tbsp.	chopped fresh oregano	15 mL
1 tbsp.	chopped fresh flat-leaf parsley	15 mL

- Preheat oven to 375˚F (190˚C).
- Heat the olive oil in a 9-inch (23-cm) skillet over medium heat. Add the garlic and cook for 1 minute, stirring frequently. Do not let the garlic burn.
- Add the onion and cook until soft. Add the tomato sauce and simmer 3–4 minutes. Remove from heat and set aside.
- Slice the zucchini into ¼-inch (0.5-cm) rounds.
- Pour the beaten eggs into a shallow dish. (A pie plate is ideal.)
- Measure the flour into another shallow dish. Season with salt and pepper.
- Mix ¾ of the Parmesan cheese with the oregano and parsley in a third shallow dish.
- Quickly dredge the zucchini rounds in the seasoned flour and shake off any excess. Do not let them sit in the flour mix.
- Dip the floured slices in the beaten eggs. Drain lightly, then dust the slices on both sides with Parmesan cheese. Set coated slices aside on a baking sheet.
- When all slices are coated, warm the remaining olive oil in a 10-inch (25-cm) skillet over medium heat.
- Sauté the discs 1–2 minutes on each side; return the slices to the baking sheet.
- Spread a thin layer of the tomato sauce in an ovenproof baking dish. Place a layer of zucchini slices on top of the sauce. Spread another layer of tomato sauce and layer with remaining slices. Finish the top with any remaining sauce and sprinkle with the rest of the Parmesan cheese.
- Bake for 15–20 minutes. Allow the casserole to cool slightly before serving.

Chef's notes: Substitute 1 tsp. (5 mL) dried oregano if fresh oregano is not available.

Garden Casserole with Herb Biscuit Topping

Makes 8–10 servings

Nutritional data per 250-g serving: Calories 240; fat 12 g; sodium 710 mg; carbohydrates 22 g; dietary fibre 3 g.

4 cups	grated zucchini	1 L
1	large red onion, finely diced	1
6	green onions	6
2	medium carrots, grated	2
4	medium tomatoes, thinly sliced	4
⅓ cup	grated Parmesan cheese	85 mL
	salt and pepper, to taste	
3	eggs	3
1½ cups	milk	375 mL
1½ cups	biscuit mix	375 mL
2 tbsp.	chopped fresh parsley	30 mL
2 tbsp.	chopped fresh chives	30 mL

- Preheat oven to 400°F (200°C). Lightly grease a 12x9-inch (30x20-cm) baking dish.
- Cover the base of the dish with the grated zucchini. Sprinkle the onion, green onions, and carrots on top of the zucchini. Layer with the tomato slices. Sprinkle cheese over vegetables; season with salt and pepper.
- In a large bowl, blend the eggs, milk, biscuit mix, parsley, and chives with a whisk or electric beater. Pour batter over vegetables.
- Bake casserole for 15 minutes. Reduce oven temperature to 350°F (175°C) and bake for an additional 20 minutes. Test for doneness by inserting a knife in the centre of the casserole.
- Serve hot.

Chef's notes: This is an excellent way to use up cooked vegetables like cauliflower, broccoli, and green beans or drained canned vegetables like chick peas, green or yellow beans, and kernel corn. Add them to the vegetable layers.

Rustic Pie

Makes 4–6 servings

*Nutritional data per 250-g serving: Calories 410; fat 33 g;
sodium 1150 mg; carbohydrates 8 g; dietary fibre 2 g.*

3 tbsp.	vegetable oil	45 mL
4	small zucchini, thinly sliced	4
1	medium red onion, finely chopped	1
½ cup	chopped fresh parsley	125 mL
2 tbsp.	chopped chives	30 mL
1 tbsp.	chopped fresh oregano	15 mL
3	large eggs	3
1½ cup	grated cheddar cheese	375 mL
½ cup	grated Parmesan cheese	125 mL
9-inch	pie crust	20-cm

- Preheat oven to 375°F (190°C).
- Heat vegetable oil in a large skillet over medium heat. Sauté the zucchini and onions for 7–8 minutes. Add the chopped herbs; cook for 1 more minute. Remove from heat and allow to cool.
- In a large bowl, mix the eggs and cheeses. Add the cooled cooked zucchini to the egg mixture; mix well.
- Pour the mixture into the pie shell. Bake on the lowest rack of the oven for 20 minutes. Serve hot.

Chef's notes: Mixed green salad makes an excellent accompaniment to this dish.
- To save time, use a frozen commercially prepared pie crust.

Zucchini Pie

Makes 6–8 servings

Nutritional data per 100-g serving: Calories 55; fat 2 g; sodium 730 mg; carbohydrates 5 g; dietary fibre 1 g.

3 cups	grated zucchini	750 mL
3	large eggs, beaten	3
½ cup	instant potato flakes	125 mL
	salt and pepper, to taste	
	olive oil for pan	
8	pitted black olives, chopped	8
2	small Roma tomatoes, diced	2
2 tbsp.	chopped fresh basil leaves	30 mL
⅓ cup	grated mozzarella cheese	85 mL

- Preheat oven to 375°F (190°C).
- In a medium bowl, mix the grated zucchini with the beaten eggs. Add the instant potato flakes, salt, and pepper; mix well.
- Generously grease a 9-inch (23-cm) glass pie plate with olive oil. Form the zucchini mix into a crust on the pie plate. Bake 20 minutes.
- Remove pie from oven and top with the olives, tomato, fresh basil, and cheese.
- Raise the oven temperature to 400°F (200°C) and bake the pie until the cheese is melted, approximately 5–6 minutes. Remove pie from oven, cut into wedges, and serve hot.

Chef's notes: Add others toppings such as tomato sauce, pre-cooked seafood or meat, sausages, and peppers.

Zucchini Phyllo Roll

Makes 4–6 servings

Nutritional data per 160-g serving: Calories 260 ; fat 17 g;
sodium 390 mg; carbohydrates 16 g; dietary fibre 12 g.

1 tbsp.	extra-virgin olive oil	15 mL
½ cup	finely diced yellow onion	125 mL
1	garlic clove, minced	1
2 cups	grated zucchini	500 mL
1 cup	fresh white bread crumbs	250 mL
1 cup	grated cheddar cheese	250 mL
½ cup	crumbled feta cheese	125 mL
8	fresh basil leaves, chopped	8
	freshly ground black pepper, to taste	
1	large egg	1
3 sheets	phyllo dough	3 sheets
2 tbsp.	butter	30 mL

• Preheat oven to 375°F (190°C).
• In a 9-inch (23-cm) skillet, heat the olive oil over medium heat. Add the chopped onion and garlic. Sauté 3–4 minutes, until tender. Remove from heat and set aside to cool.
• In a large bowl, mix together the grated zucchini, bread crumbs, cheddar cheese, feta cheese, basil, and pepper.
• Beat the egg and combine with the other ingredients. Add the cooled garlic and onions. Mix well.
• In a small bowl, melt the butter.
• Lay one sheet of phyllo dough on a counter or cutting board. Brush with melted butter. Place the second sheet of phyllo on top of the first; brush with melted butter. Repeat with the third sheet.
• Spoon the filling onto the phyllo dough, forming a log-shaped strip, leaving a 2-inch (5-cm) space at each end. Fold the phyllo dough over the filling to form a roll; seal. Close the two ends by folding the excess dough to the middle. Turn the seam to the bottom.
• Place the roll on a baking sheet. Brush with remaining melted butter.
• Bake for 20–25 minutes. Cool for 10 minutes before slicing.

Chef's notes: For best results, cut the roll with a serrated knife.

Zucchini Wraps

Makes 4 servings

Nutritional data per 215-g serving: Calories 230; fat 12 g; sodium 730 mg; carbohydrates 28 g; dietary fibre 5 g.

1 tbsp.	vegetable oil	15 mL
1	small red onion, thinly sliced	1
1 tbsp.	grated ginger root	15 mL
1 tsp.	chili powder	5 mL
¼ tsp.	dry mustard powder	1 mL
¼ tsp.	ground cloves	1 mL
¼ tsp.	ground cinnamon	1 mL
4 cups	grated zucchini	1 L
	salt and pepper, to taste	
4 10-inch	flour tortillas	4 25-cm
1 cup	guacamole	250 mL

- In a 10-inch (25-cm) sauté pan, heat the oil over medium heat. Add the onion and sauté until soft, about 3–4 minutes. Add the ginger; cook for 1 minute. Stir in the dry spices and reduce heat to medium-low.
- Add the grated zucchini; cook for 8-10 minutes, until the zucchini is soft. Season with salt and pepper.
- Grill the tortilla shells on both sides to warm them.
- Divide the zucchini mixture onto the tortillas. Roll the tortillas to enclose the filling.
- Serve with guacamole on the side.

Chef's notes: You can serve tomato salsa, minted chutney (see page 138), or sour cream along with or in place of the guacamole.

World's Best Pizza Dough

Makes 2 large pizza crusts

2 packages	dry active yeast	20 g
1 tsp.	granulated sugar	5 mL
1 cup	lukewarm water	250 mL
3½ cup	all-purpose flour	875 mL
1 tsp.	salt	5 mL
¼ cup	olive oil	65 mL
	olive oil for bowl	

- In a medium bowl, stir together the yeast, sugar, and water until the yeast is dissolved. Let mixture stand in a warm, draft-free place until the yeast starts to foam. It should double in volume. The yeast must be fresh and the water should be about 180°F (90°C)—if it's too hot, it will kill the yeast.
- In a electric mixer bowl, combine the sifted flour and salt. Add the fermented yeast and olive oil. Mix at low speed with the paddle attachment until all the ingredients are well blended.
- Change the paddle attachment to the dough hook and mix at medium speed for 7–8 minutes.
- Coat a clean bowl with olive oil. Place the dough in the oiled bowl. Cover with plastic wrap or put the bowl and dough inside a small plastic bag and keep in a warm place for about an hour. The dough will be ready to work after it has doubled in size.
- Punch the fermented dough down, and it will be ready to use.

To make the dough by hand

In a large bowl, sift together the flour and salt. Make a crater in the centre of the flour and pour in the fermented yeast mixture. Add the olive oil. Mix until the dough forms a ball.

- Knead the dough in the bowl or on the countertop until it is smooth (about 8–10 minutes). Try to keep the dough as warm as possible, as it will take longer to proof if it gets cold.
- Coat a clean bowl with olive oil. Place the dough in the oiled bowl. Cover with plastic wrap or put the bowl and dough inside a small plastic bag and keep in a warm place for about an hour. The dough will be ready to work after it has doubled in size.
- Punch the fermented dough down, and it will be ready to use.

Chef's notes: The dough can be seasoned by adding a blend of dry or freshly chopped herbs. Rosemary, basil, oregano, marjoram, and thyme are all good choices; experiment to find the blend you like best. • Thanks to Pascal and Gino at L'Etale in Morzine for the best thin-crust, wood oven-baked pizza in the world!

Fresh Zucchini Pizza

Makes 2 large pizzas

Nutritional data per 435-g serving: Calories 480; fat 25 g; sodium 1700 mg; carbohydrates 21 g; dietary fibre 2 g.

1 batch	fresh pizza dough (see page 104)	1 batch
1½ cups	tomato sauce	375 mL
1 cup	grated zucchini	250 mL
½ cup	chopped mixed fresh herbs	125 mL
2⅔ cups	grated mozzarella	675 mL
1 cup	Parmesan cheese	250 mL
	cornmeal for pans	

- Preheat oven to 400°F (200°C).
- Roll or stretch the pizza dough on a floured counter into 2 rough rounds.
- Sprinkle baking sheet or pizza pan with cornmeal. Place shaped dough on pan.
- Spread tomato sauce evenly over pizza base. Sprinkle each base with zucchini and herbs. Top with cheeses.
- Bake for 8–10 minutes on the lowest rack in the oven. Remove from oven, cut into points, and serve immediately.

Chef's notes: For individual pizzas, divide the dough into 8 equal pieces and form into rough rounds, then proceed as directed. • You can freely adapt and add to this basic method. After spreading the tomato sauce, zucchini, and herbs, add your favourite toppings. Pepperoni, ham, mushrooms, green peppers, sun-dried tomatoes, or fresh tomatoes are all great choices.

Did you know...?

A novelty variety of zucchini, called 'Eight Ball,' produces round, baseball-sized fruit.

Zucchini Calzone

Makes 8 servings

Nutritional data per 120-g serving: Calories 110; fat 7 g;
sodium 390 mg; carbohydrates 5 g; dietary fibre 5 g.

1	pizza dough recipe (see page 104)	1
2	small zucchini	2
1 cup	medium salsa, chunky style	250 mL
12	pitted black or green olives, chopped	12
6	large basil leaves, chopped	6
1/3 cup	grated mozzarella	85 mL
1 tbsp.	olive oil	15 mL
	cornmeal for baking sheet	

- Prepare pizza dough as directed. Divide dough into 8 small rounds, about 6–8 inches (15–20 cm) in diameter; the rounds should be thin.
- Preheat oven to 375°F (190°C).
- Cut zucchini into 1/4-inch (0.5-cm) slices.
- Mix zucchini, salsa, olives, basil, and mozzarella n a small bowl to form calzone filling.
- Spread filling on one half of each dough round. Don't overfill!
- Fold the top half of the dough over the filling to meet the bottom edge. Crimp the edge to form a sealed package, then brush with olive oil.
- Make a small hole in the top of each calzone to allow steam to escape during baking.
- Sprinkle cornmeal on a baking sheet. Place calzones on baking sheet and bake for 8–10 minutes.
- Serve hot or cold.

Chef's notes: Try calzones with sliced mushrooms, chopped spinach, grated cheddar cheese, or crumbled feta cheese. • Calzones freeze well. Store them in sealed, dated freezer bags. They make great lunches and after-school snacks.

Mini Zucchini Pizza

Makes 8 servings

Nutritional data per 160-serving: Calories 320; fat 27 g;
sodium 1270 mg; carbohydrates 8 g; dietary fibre 1 g.

1 batch	fresh pizza dough (see page 104)	1 batch
1	medium unpeeled zucchini	1
2 tbsp.	olive oil	30 mL
1 tbsp.	Italian herb seasoning	15 mL
1 cup	ricotta cheese	250 mL
3 tbsp.	grated Parmesan cheese	45 mL
2 tbsp.	chopped fresh basil	30 mL
1 cup	chunky tomato sauce	250 mL
2 tbsp.	sun-dried tomatoes, chopped	30 mL
½ cup	grated mozzarella cheese	125 mL
	salt and pepper, to taste	
	cornmeal for pie plate	

- Divide pizza dough into 8 portions. Roll out 1 portion ¼ inch (0.5 cm) thick to fit a 9-inch (23-cm) pie plate; brush with olive oil. Sprinkle plate with cornmeal; place shaped dough on plate. (Shape the remaining dough into rounds, seal in plastic wrap, and freeze flat for mini pizzas or calzones.)
- Preheat oven to 375°F (190°C).
- Cut the zucchini lengthwise into ¼-inch (0.5-cm) strips. Brush with olive oil and sprinkle with Italian seasoning. Grill according to method on page 25. Let strips cool.
- In a medium bowl, mix together the ricotta cheese, Parmesan cheese, and basil; set aside.
- Spread the dough base with 2 tbsp. (30 mL) of tomato sauce. Layer grilled zucchini strips on each base. Spread a layer of the seasoned cheese on the zucchini. Add another layer of grilled zucchini strips. Sprinkle chopped sun-dried tomatoes on top of the strips. Cover with mozzarella cheese.
- Bake for 30 minutes on lowest rack. Cool for 10 minutes before slicing into 8 wedges; serve warm.

Chef's notes: Here are some great possible additions: thin-sliced Roma tomatoes; sliced pitted black olives; chopped anchovies; pesto; roasted peppers. Just add these ingredients with the other layers.

Sweet Treats
and Baked Goods

Harvest Time

Pick zucchini fruit twice a week to keep the plants producing. Harvest fruits early, when they are 10–20 cm long and 5–7 cm in diameter. Zucchini are at their most tender and flavourful when picked young. If the fruit grow too large, the plant will stop producing new, smaller fruit, so pick regularly. Remember that zucchini blossoms are also edible; you can harvest and eat the blossoms and baby zucchini if the plant is producing too many fruit.

Zucchini are best used fresh, although fresh zucchini will keep in the refrigerator for about one week. You can store fully grown, mature fruits in a cold room; here they will last one or two months.

Composition of a 100-g sample of zucchini

Water	Calories	Protein	Fat	Carbohydrate
95%	15	1.2 g	0.1 g	3.6 g

Vitamin A	Vitamin C	Thiamin	Riboflavin	Niacin
32 I.U.	19 mg	0.05 mg	0.09 mg	1.0 mg

Calcium	Phosphorus	Iron	Sodium	Potassium
28 mg	29 mg	0.4 mg	1 mg	202 mg

Baked Apples with Dried Fruit

Makes 8 servings

*Nutritional data per 90-g serving: Calories 190; fat 6 g;
sodium 15 mg; carbohydrates 36 g; dietary fibre 3 g.*

2 tbsp.	golden raisins	30 mL
2 tbsp.	dried apricots, chopped	30 mL
4	Granny Smith apples	4
2 tbsp.	dried figs, chopped	30 mL
2 tbsp.	grated zucchini	30 mL
½ cup	dark brown sugar, lightly packed	125 mL
1 tsp.	grated lemon peel	5 mL
1 tsp.	grated orange peel	5 mL
2 tsp.	ground cinnamon	10 mL
1 tsp.	ground cloves	5 mL
1 tbsp.	butter	15 mL
3 tbsp.	pure maple syrup	45 mL

• Preheat oven to 350°F (190°C).
• In a small bowl, soak the raisins and apricots in hot (not boiling) water for 8–10 minutes.
• Cut apples in half lengthwise. Trim a thin slice from the base of each apple half to allow it to stand without rolling. Use a paring knife to make some small holes in the skin of the apples. With a melon-baller, remove the core and seeds of the apples. Place the apples in an oven-proof dish.
• Drain the soaked fruit and dry gently with a paper towel.
• In a medium bowl, combine figs and zucchini with the fruit mix. Add the brown sugar, orange and lemon peels, and spices; mix well.
• Fill the hollow apple centres with the fruit mix (it does not matter if the mixture spills out). Top each apple with a piece of butter.
• Drizzle the apples with maple syrup; cover and bake for 35–40 minutes, or until the apples are tender. Serve hot or cold.

Chef's notes: This recipe is best served hot with cold whipping cream or ice cream. • This dessert is a good way to use up grated zucchini left over from other recipes. • Dried cranberries are a nice addition to this recipe—they add a pleasant tartness and extra nutrition.

Zucchini-Lime Crisp

Makes 18 servings

Nutritional data per 75-g serving: Calories 210; fat 9 g; sodium 150 mg; carbohydrates 33 g; dietary fibre 0 g.

4 cups	all-purpose flour	1 L
2 cups	granulated sugar	500 mL
1 tsp.	salt	5 mL
¾ lb.	soft butter	375 mL
8 cups	zucchini, peeled, cored, and sliced 1/4 inch thick	2 L
⅔ cups	lime juice	170 mL
1	entire lime rind, grated	1
½ cup	granulated sugar	125 mL
⅔ cup	brown sugar	190 mL
3 tsp.	ground cinnamon, divided	15 mL
pinch	allspice	pinch

- Preheat oven to 350°F (175°C). Lightly grease a 9x12-inch (22x30-cm) baking dish.
- In a large bowl, mix together the flour, sugar, and salt. Cut in the butter until the mixture is crumbly.
- Using the base of a drinking glass, press ½ this mixture into the bottom of the baking dish. Reserve the remaining mixture.
- Bake the base for 8–10 minutes. Remove from the oven and cool on a wire rack.
- In a 10-inch sauté pan, cook the sliced zucchini in the lime juice over medium heat for 8 minutes, until the zucchini is tender. Add the lime rind and cook for 1 minute. Add the white and brown sugar, 1½ tsp. (7.5 mL) of the cinnamon, and the allspice; cook for 1 minute.
- Add 1/2 the reserved pastry mix to the zucchini filling and cook, stirring constantly, until the mixture thickens. Remove from heat and allow to cool. Pour filling over the top of the baked base.
- Add the remaining 1½ tsp. (7.5 mL) cinnamon to the remaining pastry mixture; stir gently. Sprinkle the mixture evenly over the top of the filling.
- Bake on the top rack of the oven for 40–45 minutes, until the top is crisp and lightly browned.

Chef's notes: This dessert is best served with whipping cream, ice cream, or vanilla custard.

Zucchini Squares

Makes 18 servings

Nutritional data per 60-g serving: Calories 220; fat 16 g; sodium 180 mg; carbohydrates 17 g; dietary fibre 2 g.

2 cups	grated unpeeled zucchini	500 mL
1½ tsp.	salt	7.5 mL
2 cups	all-purpose flour	500 mL
2 tsp.	baking powder	10 mL
½ tsp.	baking soda	2.5 mL
1 tsp.	salt	5 mL
⅔ cup	soft butter	170 mL
3	large eggs	3
2 tsp.	vanilla	10 mL
1 cup	chocolate chips	250 mL
1 cup	chopped pecans	250 mL

- In a medium bowl, mix the grated zucchini with 1½ tsp. (7.5 mL) salt; let stand at room temperature for 15 minutes. Strain the mixture through a single layer of cheesecloth to remove excess liquid. Set the strained zucchini aside.
- Preheat oven to 350°F (175°C). Lightly grease a 9x12-inch (20x30-cm) baking dish.
- In a medium bowl, mix together the flour, baking powder, baking soda, and salt.
- In a large bowl, cream the butter and sugar with an electric mixer mix until light and fluffy, about 3–4 minutes. Add the eggs and mix slowly until fully incorporated. Add the vanilla.
- Stir in the flour mixture. Add the drained zucchini, pecans, and chocolate chips; mix well.
- Pour the batter into the prepared baking dish, spreading it evenly. Bake dish on the middle rack of the oven for 30 minutes. Test for doneness with a wooden skewer.
- Cool and cut into squares.

Chef's notes: If you use a glass dish, reduce the oven temperature to 325°F (160°C).

Chocolate-Almond-Zucchini Cake

Makes 18 servings

*Nutritional data per 75-g serving: Calories 270; fat 13 g;
sodium 135 mg; carbohydrates 37 g; dietary fibre 1 g.*

1½ cup	granulated sugar	375 mL
½ cup	soft butter	125 mL
¼ cup	vegetable oil	65 mL
1 tsp.	almond extract	5 mL
2	large eggs	2
2½ cups	all-purpose flour	625 mL
¼ cup	cocoa	65 mL
1 tsp.	baking soda	5 mL
2 tsp.	ground cinnamon	10 mL
½ cup	buttermilk	125 mL
2 tsp.	finely grated orange peel	10 mL
2 cup	grated zucchini	500 mL
1 cup	chocolate chips	1 cup
½ cup	chopped almonds	125 mL

- Preheat oven to 350˚F (175˚C). Lightly grease a 9x12-inch (22x30-cm) baking dish.
- In a large bowl, beat together with an electric mixer the sugar, butter, oil, and almond extract. Add the eggs and beat until the mixture is light and creamy, about 4–5 minutes.
- Add the flour, cocoa, baking soda, cinnamon, orange peel, and buttermilk. Mix well, scraping down the sides of the bowl.
- Fold in the zucchini, chocolate chips, and almonds. Mix until all ingredients are well blended. Pour mixture into the baking dish.
- Bake on the middle rack of the oven for 35–40 minutes. Test for doneness with a small knife; if the knife comes out clean the cake is cooked. Don't overbake: this cake should be moist and tender.

Zucchini-Pear Cobbler

Makes about 12 servings

Nutritional data per 110-g serving: Calories 180; fat 7 g; sodium 0 mg; carbohydrates 29 g; dietary fibre 2 g.

4 cups	Anjou pears, peeled, diced, and cored	1 L
4 cups	zucchini, peeled, seeded, and sliced	1 L
3 tbsp.	lemon juice	45 mL
3 tbsp.	lime juice	45 mL
1 tsp.	ground cinnamon	5 mL
½ tsp.	ground cloves	2.5 mL
½ tsp.	nutmeg	2.5 mL
1 cup	granulated sugar	250 mL
4 cups	all-purpose flour	1 L
2 cups	granulated sugar	500 mL
1½ cups	cold butter	375 mL
2 tsp.	ground cinnamon	10 mL
3 tbsp.	granulated sugar	45 mL

- In a large saucepan over medium heat, stir together the pears, zucchini, lemon juice, and lime juice. Bring to a boil and reduce heat. Cook for 15–20 minutes, until pears and zucchini are tender.
- Add 1 tsp. (5 mL) cinnamon, cloves, nutmeg and 1 cup (250 mL) sugar. Cook for 2 minutes, then remove from heat.
- Preheat oven to 375°F (190°C).
- In a large bowl, mix the flour and 2 cups (500 mL) sugar. Cut in the butter until the mixture form a coarse crumb texture. Stir in ½ cup (125 mL) of the zucchini-pear mixture.
- Using the base of a drinking glass, press half the crumb mixture into the base of a 9x13-inch (22x33-cm) baking dish.
- Spread the remaining zucchini/pear mix over the base. Sprinkle the remaining crumb mix over the filling.
- Combine 2 tsp. (10 mL) cinnamon and 3 tbsp. (45 mL) sugar. Sprinkle over the crumb topping.
- Bake cobbler on the middle oven rack for 40 minutes, until golden-brown.

Chocolate-Zucchini Brownies

Makes 16 servings

Nutritional data per 65-g serving: Calories 210; fat 11 g; sodium 115 mg; carbohydrates 25 g; dietary fibre 1 g.

10-oz.	packaged brownie mix	310-g
1	large egg	1
¼ cup	water	65 mL
2 tbsp.	butter	30 mL
½ cup	chopped walnuts	125 mL
1 cup	grated zucchini	250 mL

- Preheat oven to 350˚F (175˚C). Lightly grease a 8x8-inch (20x20-cm) baking dish.
- Empty the brownie mix into a medium bowl. Add the egg, water, butter, and walnuts; mix all ingredients with a spoon. Add the grated zucchini and mix well.
- Pour the mix into the baking dish. Bake for 30–35 minutes or until the brownies are almost set in the centre.

Chef's notes: This recipe makes very moist brownies—kids will love them!

Zucchini Cookies

Makes about 24 cookies

Nutritional data per 35-g serving: Calories 120; fat 5 g; sodium 95 mg; carbohydrates 19 g; dietary fibre 0 g.

1 cup	brown sugar	250 mL
1 cup	granulated sugar	250 mL
½ cup	shortening	125 mL
½ cup	soft butter	125 mL
2	large eggs	2
2 cups	grated zucchini	500 mL
3½ cups	all-purpose flour	875 mL
1 tsp.	baking soda	5 mL
1 tsp.	salt	5 mL
1 tsp.	ground cinnamon	5 mL

- Preheat oven to 350°F (175°C). Grease cookie sheets.
- In a large bowl, cream together brown sugar, granulated sugar, shortening, and butter. Add the eggs one at a time; mix well. Add the zucchini; stir.
- In a medium bowl, mix together flour, baking soda, salt, and cinnamon.
- Add the dry ingredients to the moist ingredients. Mix until fully incorporated.
- Drop the cookies by spoonfuls onto cookie sheets. Bake 10–12 minutes.
- Remove cookies from pan with a spatula and cool on a wire rack.

Zucchini-Oatmeal Cookies

Makes about 24 cookies

Nutritional data per 35-g serving: Calories 140; fat 8 g; sodium 120 mg; carbohydrates 16 g; dietary fibre 1 g.

½ cup	shortening	125 mL
1	large egg	1
⅓ cup	honey	85 mL
pinch	baking soda	pinch
1 cup	all-purpose flour	250 mL
1 tsp.	baking powder	5 mL
¼ tsp.	salt	1 mL
1 cup	rolled oats	250 mL
½ cup	grated unpeeled zucchini	125 mL
½ cup	chopped pecans or cashews	125 mL
½ cup	golden raisins	125 mL
1 tsp.	vanilla extract	5 mL

- Preheat oven to 350°F (175°C). Grease cookie sheets.
- In a large mixing bowl with an electric mixer, cream together the shortening and egg.
- In a small bowl, mix together the honey and baking soda; add to the creamed mixture.
- In a medium bowl, sift together the flour, baking powder and salt; add to the wet ingredients until well incorporated.
- Stir in the rolled oats, zucchini, nuts, and raisins. Add the vanilla and stir well.
- Drop cookies onto greased sheets. Flatten slightly with a floured fork. Bake 10–12 minutes, until lightly golden.
- Remove cookies with a flat spatula and let cool on a wire rack.

Homestyle Cookies

Makes about 12 cookies

*Nutritional data per 35-g serving: Calories 110; fat 4 g;
sodium 120 mg; carbohydrates 19 g; dietary fibre 2 g.*

¾ cup	honey	190 mL
½ cup	soft butter	125 mL
1	large egg	1
2 cups	whole-wheat flour	500 mL
1 tsp.	baking soda	5 mL
pinch	ground cloves	pinch
1 tsp.	ground cinnamon	5 mL
½ tsp.	ground nutmeg	2.5 mL
pinch	salt	pinch
1 cup	grated zucchini	250 mL
1 cup	rolled oats	250 mL
1 cup	yellow raisins	250 mL

- Preheat oven to 375°F (190°C). Grease cookie sheets.
- In a large bowl, cream together the honey and butter with an electric mixer at medium speed for 2 minutes. Add the egg; mix for 1 minute.
- In a medium bowl, sift the flour, baking soda, spices, and salt.
- Add the zucchini alternately with the flour mix to the creamed mixture. Stir in the oats and raisins.
- Drop cookies onto a greased sheets with a spoon. Bake for 10–12 minutes.
- Remove cookies with a flat spatula; cool on a wire rack.

Zucchini-Cheese Muffins

Makes 12 muffins

*Nutritional data per 60-g serving: Calories 130; fat 6 g;
sodium 140 mg; carbohydrates 18 g; dietary fibre 3 g.*

⅔ cup	milk	85 mL
1 cup	dry bran-type cereal	250 mL
⅓ cup	sour cream	85 mL
⅓ cup	brown sugar	85 mL
⅓ cup	melted butter	85 mL
1	large egg	1
1 cup	whole-wheat flour	250 mL
2 tsp.	baking powder	10 mL
½ tsp.	baking soda	2.5 mL
1 cup	grated unpeeled zucchini	250 mL
1 cup	grated medium cheddar cheese	250 mL
1 tbsp.	grated Parmesan cheese	15 mL

- Preheat oven to 400°F (200°C). Lightly grease and line muffin tins.
- In a large bowl, pour the milk over the dry cereal and soak for 3 minutes. Stir in the sour cream. Mix in the brown sugar, melted butter, and egg.
- In a medium bowl, sift together the flour, baking powder, and baking soda. Add the dry ingredients to the wet mixture.
- Stir in the grated zucchini and cheddar cheese until well combined.
- Fill the muffin tins. Sprinkle with Parmesan cheese and bake 20 minutes, until golden-brown. Serve warm.

Applesauce-Zucchini Muffins

Makes 12 muffins

*Nutritional data per 60-g serving: Calories 170; fat 7 g;
sodium 20 mg; carbohydrates 24 g; dietary fibre 3 g.*

⅓ cup	finely diced apple	85 mL
⅔ cup	grated zucchini	170 mL
⅓ cup	vegetable oil	85 mL
⅓ cup	milk	85 mL
1 tsp.	vanilla extract	5 mL
2	large eggs	2
½ cup	brown sugar	125 mL
2 cups	whole-wheat flour	500 mL
3 tsp.	baking powder	15 mL
1 tsp.	ground cinnamon	5 mL

- Preheat oven to 350°F (175°C). Grease and line 12 muffin tins.
- In a medium bowl, mix together the apple, zucchini, vegetable oil, milk, vanilla, and eggs.
- In a large bowl, mix together the brown sugar, flour, baking powder, and cinnamon.
- Add the wet ingredients to the dry ingredients; mix until just blended.
- Fill the muffin tins and bake for 20–25 minutes. Serve warm.

Did you know...?

Many people believe that summer squashes (including zucchini) will cross-pollinate with melons and cucumbers. This is simply not true. However, varieties within each species will cross-pollinate. For example, zucchini will cross-pollinate with crookneck or acorn squash if the plants are grown in the same area.

Blueberry-Zucchini Muffins

Makes 12 muffins

Nutritional data per 60-g serving: Calories 140; fat 5 g; sodium 180 mg; carbohydrates 23 g; dietary fibre 1 g.

2	large eggs	2
²⁄₃ cups	milk	170 mL
¼ cup	melted butter	65 mL
1½ cups	all-purpose flour	375 mL
3 tsp.	baking powder	15 mL
½ tsp.	salt	2.5 mL
2 tbsp.	granulated sugar	30 mL
½ cup	blueberries	125 mL
½ cup	finely diced zucchini	125 mL
¼ cup	all-purpose flour	65 mL
½ cup	granulated sugar	125 mL

- Preheat oven to 400°F (200°C). Prepare muffin tins.
- In a medium bowl, beat together the eggs, milk, and melted butter with a whisk.
- In a large bowl, mix together 1½ cups (375 mL) flour, baking powder, salt, and 2 tbsp. (30 mL) of sugar.
- Stir the wet ingredients into the dry mix.
- In a separate bowl, mix together blueberries, zucchini, ½ cup (125 mL) sugar, and ¼ cup (65 mL) flour; fold into the batter.
- Fill muffin tins and bake for 20–25 minutes until golden-brown. Serve warm.

Spicy Zucchini Cupcakes

Makes 18–24 cupcakes

*Nutritional data per 60-g serving: Calories 110; fat 1 g;
sodium 85 mg; carbohydrates 26 g; dietary fibre 1 g.*

3	large eggs	3
1⅓ cup	granulated sugar	335 mL
2 tsp.	vegetable oil	10 mL
½ cup	orange juice	125 mL
1 tsp.	vanilla extract	5 mL
1½ cup	all-purpose flour	375 mL
2 tsp.	baking powder	10 mL
1 tsp.	ground cinnamon	5 mL
1 tsp.	ground ginger	5 mL
pinch	nutmeg	pinch
pinch	cloves	pinch
pinch	salt	pinch
1½ cups	grated zucchini	375 mL

- Preheat oven to 350°F (175°C). Line or lightly grease muffin tins.
- In a large mixing bowl, combine the eggs, sugar, vegetable oil, orange juice, and vanilla. Beat together with an electric mixer at medium-high speed for 3–4 minutes.
- In a separate bowl, combine the flour, baking powder, cinnamon, ginger, nutmeg, cloves, and salt.
- Add the dry ingredients to the egg mixture; mix well. Add the grated zucchini and mix all ingredients well with a wooden spoon.
- Fill the prepared muffin tins ¾ full. Bake on the middle rack of the oven for 20–25 minutes. Test for doneness with a toothpick. Remove from oven and allow the muffins to cool for 6–7 minutes before transferring them to a wire rack to cool completely.

Chocolate Pecan-Zucchini Loaf

Makes 2 loaves

Nutritional data per 30-g serving: Calories 100; fat 5 g; sodium 90 mg; carbohydrates 12 g; dietary fibre 1 g.

2 cups	grated zucchini	500 mL
1½ tsp.	salt	7.5 mL
3	large eggs	3
¾ cup	vegetable oil	190 mL
2 cups	granulated sugar	500 mL
2½ cups	all-purpose flour	625 mL
½ cup	cocoa	125 mL
2 tsp.	baking soda	10 mL
1 tsp.	cinnamon	5 mL
pinch	nutmeg	pinch
1 tsp.	salt	5 mL
½ cup	milk	125 mL
1 cup	chopped pecans	250 mL

- In a medium bowl, mix the grated zucchini with 1½ tsp. (7.5 mL) salt; let stand at room temperature for 15 minutes. Strain the mixture through a single layer of cheesecloth to remove excess liquid. Set the drained zucchini aside.
- Preheat oven to 350°F (175°C). Lightly grease 2 9x5-inch (23x13-cm) loaf pans.
- In a large bowl, with an electric mixer, beat together the eggs, oil, and sugar.
- In a medium bowl, mix together flour, cocoa, baking soda, cinnamon, nutmeg, and salt.
- Add the dry ingredients to the wet mixture. Add the milk; fold in the drained zucchini and pecans.
- Divide the mixture evenly between the loaf pans. Bake on the middle rack of the oven for 50 minutes. Test for doneness with a wooden skewer in the centre of the loaf. (The skewer will be clean when the loaf is cooked.)
- Let the loaves sit for 10 minutes in the pans, then turn out onto wire racks to cool completely.

Zucchini-Cranberry-Pineapple Loaf

Makes 2 loaves

Nutritional data per 55-g serving: Calories 180; fat 9 g; sodium 145 mg; carbohydrates 24 g; dietary fibre 1 g.

3	large eggs	3
2 cups	granulated sugar	500 mL
2 tsp.	orange essence	10 mL
1 cup	vegetable oil	250 mL
2 cups	grated zucchini	500 mL
1 cup	canned crushed pineapple, well drained	250 mL
3 cups	all-purpose flour	750 mL
1 tsp.	baking powder	5 mL
2 tsp.	baking soda	10 mL
1 tsp.	salt	5 mL
2 tsp.	ground cinnamon	10 mL
1 cup	chopped walnuts	250 mL
1 cup	dried cranberries	250 mL

- Preheat oven to 350°F (175°C). Lightly grease 2 9x5-inch (23x13-cm) loaf pans.
- In a large bowl, combine the eggs, sugar, orange essence, and vegetable oil. Beat with an electric mixer until the mixture is foamy and thick, about 6–8 minutes. Stir in the grated zucchini and drained pineapple.
- In a medium bowl, mix together the flour, baking powder, baking soda, salt, cinnamon, walnuts, and cranberries. Stir into the egg mixture with a wooden spoon or spatula. Don't overmix.
- Divide the batter between the loaf pans. Bake on the middle rack of the oven for 1 hour. Check for doneness with a wooden skewer or toothpick; it will come out clean when the loaf is baked.
- Cool loaves in the pans for 10 minutes, then turn out onto a wire rack to cool completely.

Chocolate and Nut Zucchini Loaf

Makes 2 loaves

Nutritional data per 60-g serving: Calories 230; fat 14 g; sodium 45 mg; carbohydrates 25 g; dietary fibre 1 g.

2 oz.	bittersweet chocolate	60 g
3	large eggs	3
1 cup	vegetable oil	250 mL
2 cups	grated peeled zucchini	500 mL
2 tsp.	almond extract	10 mL
3 cups	all-purpose flour	750 mL
1/4 tsp.	baking powder	1 mL
1/2 tsp.	baking soda	2.5 mL
1 tsp.	allspice	5 mL
2 cups	granulated sugar	500 mL
1 cup	chopped pecans	250 mL
2/3 cup	chocolate chips	190 mL

- Preheat oven to 350°F (175°C). Grease and flour 2 9x5-inch (23x13-cm) loaf pans.
- Melt the chocolate over a double-boiler.
- In a large bowl, combine the eggs and oil; mix with a wooden spoon. Add the melted chocolate. Stir in the zucchini and almond extract.
- In a separate bowl, sift together the flour, baking powder, baking soda, and allspice.
- Stir the sugar into the chocolate-zucchini mix. Stir in the flour mixture, chopped pecans, and chocolate chips; mix well.
- Divide the batter between the loaf pans. Bake for 1 hour on the middle rack of the oven. Check for doneness with a wooden skewer or toothpick; it will come out clean when the loaf is baked.
- Let the loaves cool in the pans for 10 minutes, then turn out onto a wire rack to cool completely.

Low-Fat Zucchini Loaf

Makes 3 loaves

Nutritional data per 60-g serving: Calories 140; fat 4 g;
sodium 70 mg; carbohydrates 25 g; dietary fibre 1 g.

3	eggs	3
1½ cups	granulated sugar	375 mL
1 tsp.	vanilla extract	5 mL
2 tsp.	lemon juice	10 mL
1 cup	applesauce	250 mL
2 cups	grated zucchini	500 mL
3 cups	all-purpose flour	750 mL
1 tsp.	baking powder	5 mL
1 tsp.	baking soda	5 mL
⅔ cup	canned crushed pineapple, well drained	190 mL
½ cup	chopped walnuts	125 mL
½ cup	slivered almonds	125 mL
½ cup	golden raisins	125 mL

- Preheat oven to 325°F (160°C). Grease and flour 3 8x4-inch (20x10-cm) loaf pans.
- In a large bowl, combine the eggs, sugar, vanilla, lemon juice, and applesauce. Using an electric mixer, beat until light and fluffy. With a wooden spoon, stir in the grated zucchini.
- Add the flour, baking powder, and baking soda; stir until well combined. Stir in the pineapple, chopped walnuts, almonds, and raisins.
- Divide the mixture into the prepared loaf pans. Bake for 1 hour on the middle rack of the oven. Test with a toothpick or small knife in the centre of the loaf; if it comes out clean, the cake is cooked. Let the loaves cool in the pans for 10 minutes, then turn out onto a wire rack to cool completely.

Zucchini-Ginger Loaf

Makes 1 loaf

*Nutritional data per 30-g serving: Calories 100; fat 4 g;
sodium 120 mg; carbohydrates 18 g; dietary fibre 0 g.*

¼ cup	brown sugar	65 mL
¼ cup	granulated sugar	65 mL
½ cup	vegetable oil	125 mL
1	large egg	1
1 cup	molasses	250 mL
1/2 cup	grated unpeeled zucchini	125 mL
3 cups	all-purpose flour	750 mL
1½ tsp.	baking soda	7.5 mL
1 tsp.	ground cinnamon	5 mL
1 tsp.	ground ginger	5 mL
pinch	salt	pinch
1 cup	hot water	250 mL

- Preheat oven to 350°F (175°C). Lightly grease a 12x9-inch (30x20-cm) baking dish.
- In a large bowl, beat together the sugars and the vegetable oil. Add the egg and the molasses; beat for 2 minutes. Add the grated zucchini.
- In a medium bowl, sift together flour, baking soda, cinnamon, ginger, and salt.
- Add the dry ingredients to the creamed mixture alternately with the hot water.
- Pour batter into the greased baking dish and bake for 40–45 minutes.
- Cut into squares and serve.

Chef's notes: This dessert is best served warm with fresh whipped cream, into which you have beaten a few drops of orange liqueur.

Zucchini-Coconut Quick Bread

Makes 2 loaves

*Nutritional data per 85-g serving: Calories 300; fat 14 g;
sodium 110 mg; carbohydrates 41 g; dietary fibre 1 g.*

3	large eggs	3
2 cups	granulated sugar	500 mL
1 cup	vegetable oil	250 mL
1 tsp.	vanilla extract	5 mL
3 cups	all-purpose flour	750 mL
½ tsp.	baking powder	2.5 mL
1 tsp.	baking soda	5 mL
2 tsp.	ground cinnamon	10 mL
½ tsp.	salt	2.5 mL
2 cups	grated zucchini	500 mL
2 tsp.	all-purpose flour	10 mL
⅔ cup	flaked coconut	190 mL

- Preheat oven to 350°F (175°C). Lightly grease 2 9x5-inch (23x13-cm) loaf pans.
- In a large bowl, beat the eggs, sugar, oil, and vanilla with an electric mixer until smooth and creamy, about 2–3 minutes.
- Add the 3 cups (750 mL) of flour, baking powder, baking soda, cinnamon, and salt; blend well. Stir the zucchini into the batter.
- In a medium bowl, mix coconut with 2 tsp. (10 mL) flour. Stir into the batter using a wooden spoon.
- Divide the mixture evenly between the loaf pans. Bake on the middle rack of the oven for 1 hour. Test for doneness with a small knife; if the knife comes out clean the cake is cooked. Allow the loaves to cool in the pans for 5 minutes, then turn the loaves out onto a wire rack to cool completely.

Zucchini-Apple Pie

Makes 1 9-inch (23-cm) pie

*Nutritional data per 110-g serving: Calories 200; fat 7 g;
sodium 120 mg; carbohydrates 35 g; dietary fibre 2 g.*

1	lemon, juice and grated peel	1
2 cups	grated zucchini	500 mL
4	Granny Smith apples, peeled, cored, and finely diced	4
¾ cup	granulated sugar	190 mL
1 tsp.	cinnamon	5 mL
pinch	ground cloves	pinch
¼ cup	butter	65 mL
½ cup	brown sugar	125 mL
1 cup	all-purpose flour	250 mL
9-inch	unbaked pie shell	23-cm

- Preheat oven to 400°F (200°C).
- Grate the lemon peel and squeeze the juice; set aside.
- In a large bowl, combine the zucchini, apples, white sugar, cinnamon, cloves, and reserved lemon juice and peel.
- In a medium bowl with an electric mixer at medium speed, cream together the butter and brown sugar until very light, 3–4 minutes. Mix in the flour with a wooden spoon.
- Pour the zucchini-apple mixture into the pie shell. Spread the creamed topping over the filling.
- Bake pie on the middle shelf of the oven for 45–60 minutes.

Chef's notes: If the top begins to brown too quickly, cover it lightly with aluminum foil. • This dish is best enjoyed with top-quality vanilla ice cream.

Lemon Custard Pie

Makes 1 9-inch (23-cm) pie

*Nutritional data per 110-g serving: Calories 280; fat 13 g;
sodium 310 mg; carbohydrates 41 g; dietary fibre 1 g.*

3	small zucchini	3
2	large eggs	2
1 ½ cups	white sugar	375 mL
14-oz. can	evaporated milk	398-mL can
½ cup	softened margarine	125 mL
¼ cup	all-purpose flour	65 mL
½ tsp.	salt	2.5 mL
2 tsp.	grated lemon peel	10 mL
1 tbsp.	lemon juice	15 mL
9-inch	unbaked pie shell	23-cm
1 tbsp.	cinnamon sugar	15 mL

- Peel the zucchini, remove the seeds, and slice coarsely. Steam slices for 6–7 minutes, then cool. You should have about 2 cups (500 mL) of zucchini.
- Preheat oven to 425°F (215°C).
- In a food processor, combine the cooled cooked zucchini, eggs, sugar, evaporated milk, margarine, flour, and salt; blend until smooth.
- Transfer mixture into a bowl. Mix in the lemon peel and lemon juice. Pour the mixture into the pie shell.
- Dust the filling with cinnamon sugar.
- Bake pie on the lower shelf of the oven at 425°F (215°C) for 5 minutes. Lower the temperature to 325°F (160°C), and bake for 20 minutes, until the pie is set. Test the centre with a small knife blade; if it comes out clean, the pie is done.
- Cool and serve.

Cheese and Zucchini Powder Biscuits

Makes 12–14 biscuits

Nutritional data per 25-g serving: Calories 80; fat 1 g; sodium 190 mg; carbohydrates 4 g; dietary fibre 0 g.

2¼ cups	all-purpose flour	565 mL
4 tsp.	baking powder	20 mL
½ tsp.	salt	2.5 mL
pinch	nutmeg	pinch
¾ cup	cold margarine	190 mL
½ cup	old cheddar cheese, grated	125 mL
1 tsp.	dried oregano	5 mL
½ cup	grated zucchini	125 mL
¾ cup	cold milk	190 mL
1	large egg	1
1 tbsp.	water	15 mL

- Preheat oven to 400°F (200°C).
- In a large bowl, combine flour, baking powder, salt, and nutmeg. Cut in the margarine until the mix resembles cornmeal. Stir in the cheese, oregano, and zucchini; mix well.
- Make a well in the centre of the mixture and pour in the milk. Mix the dough lightly with a fork or fingertips until it forms a ball. Gently knead the dough for 30 seconds, but don't overwork it.
- Place the dough on a floured surface and roll out ½ inch (1 cm) thick. Using a 4-inch (10-cm) straight-edge cookie cutter, cut the dough into biscuits. Do not twist the cutter. Place the biscuits on an ungreased cookie sheet.
- In a small bowl, beat the egg; add the water and mix. Brush the biscuit tops lightly with the egg-and-water mixture.
- Bake biscuits 10–12 minutes, until the biscuits are golden-brown. Serve hot with herb butter or a fresh garden salad.

Zucchini-Cornmeal Scones

Makes 6–8 servings

Nutritional data per 190-g serving: Calories 310 ; fat 11 g; sodium 230 mg; carbohydrates 46 g; dietary fibre 2 g.

¾ cup	cornmeal	190 mL
1 cup	grated zucchini	250 mL
1¼ cup	skim milk	315 mL
1 cup	all-purpose flour	250 mL
⅓ cup	sugar	85 mL
1 tbsp.	baking powder	15 mL
pinch	salt	pinch
1 tsp.	fresh sage, chopped	5 mL
1 tsp.	dried pepper flakes	5 mL
1	large egg	1
¼ cup	canola oil	65 mL

- Preheat oven to 375°F (190°C). Grease a 9-inch (23-cm) pie plate.
- In a large bowl, combine the cornmeal, grated zucchini, and milk; stir and set aside.
- In a medium bowl, combine the flour, sugar, baking powder, salt, sage, and pepper flakes. Mix well.
- Add the egg and oil to the cornmeal mixture; mix well.
- Add dry ingredients to wet ingredients and mix only until combined. Do not overmix.
- Pour the mixture into the greased pie plate. Bake for 30–35 minutes.
- Cool in the pie plate for about 10 minutes before cutting into wedges. Serve warm.

Chef's notes: You can use a pinch of dried, rubbed sage in place of fresh sage. • These scones make an excellent accompaniment to hearty dishes like chili.

Dips and
Spreads

Zucchini: The Genus

Zucchini is a squash, one of the many cultivars covered by the Latin name Cucurbita pepo *ssp.* pepo. *Zucchini is a New World plant, originating in the region occupied today by northern Mexico and the southwestern United States. In fact, 9,000-year-old* Cucurbita pepo *seeds have been discovered in Mexico's Oaxaca Valley. The genus* Cucurbita *also includes pumpkins, winter squashes, ornamental gourds, and the summer squashes like marrow and cocozelle.*

Zucchini, *the word Canadians have settled upon to describe this particular variety of summer squash, is an Italian term. The French word for zucchini is* courgette, *which is also the preferred name for the plant in both France and the United Kingdom. Americans often call zucchini "baby squash," while in Mexico, zucchini are called* calabacita.

Zucchini-Pineapple Salsa

Makes 3 cups (750 mL)

*Nutritional data per 90-g serving: Calories 30; fat 0 g;
sodium 3 mg; carbohydrates 7 g; dietary fibre 1 g.*

1	small fresh pineapple	1
	or	
1½ cups	canned diced pineapple	340-mL can
4	small Roma tomatoes, seeded and finely diced	4
2	small zucchini, finely diced	2
1	small red onion, peeled and finely diced	1
¼	red pepper, finely diced	¼
1	jalapeño pepper, seeded and finely diced	1
1	small chayote squash, finely diced	1
	hot pepper sauce, to taste	
2 tbsp.	lime juice	30 mL

- If using fresh pineapple, peel and core the pineapple and chop the fruit to measure 1½ cups. If using canned pineapple, drain the fruit.
- In a medium bowl, mix together the pineapple and the tomatoes. Add the zucchini, onion, red pepper, jalapeño pepper, and squash; mix well.
- Add a few drops of hot pepper sauce and the lime juice; mix well. Cover and let stand for 1 hour before serving.

Chef's notes: For extra flavour, add chopped fresh cilantro to taste. • Serve this salsa on the side with grilled meats, poultry, and fish. Stir into plain white rice for an unusual flavour combination.

Red Onion and Zucchini Relish

Makes 3 cups (750 mL)

*Nutritional data per 80-g serving: Calories 43; fat 0 g;
sodium 103 mg; carbohydrates 10 g; dietary fibre 1 g.*

1	large red onion, finely diced	1
2	medium zucchini, diced	2
½ cup	yellow raisins	125 mL
¼ cup	white wine	65 mL
3 tbsp.	cider vinegar	45 mL
2 tbsp.	demerara sugar	30 mL
¼ tsp.	dry chili pepper flakes	1 mL
½ tsp.	salt	2.5 mL
¾ cup	water	190 mL

- Place all ingredients in a non-corrosive medium saucepan. Bring to a boil. Reduce heat and simmer for 35–40 minutes, stirring occasionally.
- When most of the liquid is reduced and the mixture is slightly thickened, remove from heat and allow to cool.
- Ladle into glass or plastic containers and refrigerate.

Chef's notes: This relish will keep well for up to 3 weeks in the refrigerator.

Did you know...?

Gardeners are often concerned when many flowers appear on the plant early in its growth but no fruit set. This is usually because the early flowers are all male. Female flowers develop later and can be identified by the miniature fruit at the base of the flower. However, in hybrid varieties, the first flowers are normally female, and they will fail to develop unless there are male flowers in the area—along with bees to transfer the pollen.

Zucchini Chutney

Makes 6 cups (1.5 L)

Nutritional data per 60-g serving: Calories 70; fat 0 g;
sodium 0 mg; carbohydrates 17 g; dietary fibre 1 g.

6 cups	grated zucchini	1.5 L
1 cup	clover honey	250 mL
1⅓ cup	balsamic vinegar	335 mL
½ cup	diced yellow onion	125 mL
1½ cup	chopped dried figs	375 mL
2	medium red peppers, finely diced	2
2	Granny Smith apples, peeled, cored, and grated	2
1	lime, juice plus grated rind	1
⅓ cup	mango purée	85 mL
1	cinnamon stick	1

- Combine all ingredients in a large stainless pot. Bring to a boil. Reduce heat to medium and cook, uncovered, until thick, about 35–40 minutes.
- Remove from heat; cool. Store in the refrigerator in a non-corrosive container with a tight-fitting lid.

Chef's notes: The chutney will keep well for 3 weeks in the refrigerator. This recipe can be made in bulk for canning using the traditional canning procedure.
- The cinnamon stick will continue to infuse flavour if it is left in the chutney. For less intense flavour, remove the stick after cooking.

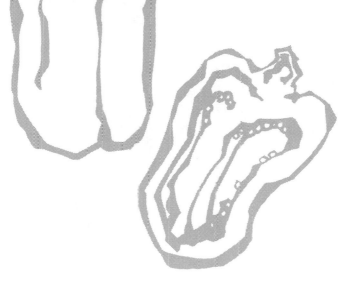

Minted Chutney

Makes 3 cups (750 mL)

*Nutritional data per 90-g serving: Calories 60; fat 0 g;
sodium 140 mg; carbohydrates 13 g; dietary fibre 1 g.*

3 lbs.	zucchini, finely diced	1.3 kg
2 tsp.	salt	10 mL
2	small yellow onions, finely diced	2
2	Granny Smith apples, finely diced	2
1 tbsp.	grated ginger root	15 mL
1 cup	dark raisins	250 mL
1 cup	packed yellow sugar	250 mL
3½ cups	malt vinegar	875 mL
½ cup	finely chopped fresh mint leaves	125 mL

• Place diced zucchini in a ceramic bowl. Sprinkle with salt and mix well. Cover with plastic wrap and refrigerate overnight.

• Rinse the marinated zucchini and drain well.

• In a heavy-bottomed medium saucepan, combine all the ingredients. Bring the mixture to a boil over medium-high heat. Reduce heat the medium-low and cook mixture until it is slightly thickened and there is no excess liquid.

• Transfer the mix into glass or non-corrosive containers with tight-fitting lids. Store in the fridge.

Chef's notes: Make this recipe in bulk at harvest time and store for use at Christmas. Use the traditional canning method once the mixture is cooked.
• Serve chutney with lamb, roast turkey, or baked ham.

Quick Zucchini Dip

Makes 2½ cups (625 mL)

Nutritional data per 100-g serving: Calories 50; fat 4 g;
sodium 25 mg; carbohydrates 5 g; dietary fibre 1 g.

3	small zucchini	3
½ cup	sour cream	125 mL
½ cup	plain yogourt	125 mL
1½ tbsp.	lime juice	7.5 mL
1 tbsp.	chopped fresh dil	15 mL

• Peel the zucchini and place in a microwave-safe medium bowl. Cover and cook for 3 minutes. Remove the cover and drain any excess liquid. Allow the zucchini to cool.
• Mix together the sour cream and yogourt in a medium bowl.
• Finely chop the cooked zucchini with a sharp knife. Add to the yogourt-sour cream mix.
• Add the lime juice and dill. Cover and refrigerate for 1 hour before serving.

Chef's notes: Serve as a salad dressing on mixed greens or as a dip with pita chips or pita bread. • This recipe makes a great side dish with grilled fish or curry.

Fresh Vegetable Dip

Makes 2½ cups (625 mL)

*Nutritional data per 30-g serving: Calories 13; fat 1 g;
sodium 26 mg; carbohydrates 1 g; dietary fibre 0 g.*

1½ cups	grated zucchini	375 mL
2 tsp.	salt	10 mL
1 cup	plain yogourt	250 mL
2 tbsp.	grated Parmesan cheese	30 mL
1 tsp.	lime juice	5 mL
2	cloves garlic, minced	2
2 tsp.	chopped fresh basil	10 mL
2	whole green onions, finely diced	2
	salt and pepper, to taste	

- Place the grated zucchini in a large glass bowl. Sprinkle with salt and mix well. Let mixture stand at room temperature for 1 hour.
- In a medium bowl, combine the remaining ingredients. Cover with plastic wrap and refrigerate while the zucchini is draining.
- Strain the zucchini through a single layer of cheesecloth and squeeze out all excess moisture.
- Add the zucchini to the yogourt mix; chill dip overnight.

Chef's notes: This recipe tastes best when it's made with freshly grated, good-quality Parmesan cheese. Low-fat yogourt can be used as a substitute for whole-milk yogourt. • Serve this dip with melba toast or toasted baguette slices, or as a side dish with a fresh vegetable platter.

Zucchini Pickles

Makes 3 cups (750 mL)

*Nutritional data per 90-g serving. Calories 20; fat 0 g;
sodium 25 mg; carbohydrates 5 g; dietary fibre 1 g.*

1¼ cups	water	315 mL
1¼ cups	cider vinegar	315 mL
1 tsp.	sea salt	5 mL
2 tbsp.	yellow mustard seed	30 mL
12	tricolour peppercorns	12
1	bay leaf	1
4	small zucchini, cut into thin slices	4
1	medium red onion, cut into rings	1
1	medium red or yellow pepper, cut into small dice	1
2	cloves garlic, chopped	2
2 tbsp.	chopped fresh dill	30 mL

- In a large saucepan, combine the water, vinegar, salt, mustard seed, peppercorns, and bay leaf. Bring to a boil and simmer uncovered for 10 minutes.
- In a large glass bowl, combine the zucchini, onion, pepper, and garlic. Mix well.
- Pour the hot marinade over the vegetables. Sprinkle the chopped dill over the vegetables.
- Allow to cool for 20 minutes at room temperature. Cover with plastic wrap and refrigerate.

Chef's notes: These pickles will keep well for 1 week in the refrigerator. • Use these pickles as a topping for mixed green salad—they're very colourful!

Quick Zucchini-Ginger Jam

Makes 6 cups (1.5 L)

Nutritional data per 20-g serving: Calories 45; fat 0 g;
sodium 0 mg; carbohydrates 12 g; dietary fibre 0g.

6 cups	grated peeled zucchini	1.5 L
6 cups	granulated sugar	1.5 L
½ cup	lemon juice	125 mL
	grated rind of 1 lemon	
1 cup	crushed pineapple with juice	250 mL
1 tbsp.	grated ginger root	15 mL
6 oz.	lemon-flavoured gelatin powder	180 g

- In a large stainless saucepan over medium-high heat, bring the zucchini to a boil. (It will make its own juice.) Cook for 5–6 minutes.
- Add sugar, lemon juice, lemon rind, crushed pineapple and juice, and the grated ginger. Boil for another 5 minutes.
- Remove from heat and add the gelatin powder; stir until the gelatin is dissolved.
- Pour mixture into sealable containers. The jam will keep for 3 months in the refrigerator.

Chef's notes: I like this jam on toasted English muffins with lots of butter!

Zucchini Paté

Yields 1½ cups (375 mL)

Nutritional data per 30-g serving: Calories 35; fat 3 g; sodium 175 mg; carbohydrates 1 g; dietary fibre 1 g.

2	small zucchini, grated	2
1 tbsp.	Japanese rice vinegar	15 mL
1 tsp.	sugar	5 mL
1 tsp.	salt	5 mL
¼ cup	chopped fresh parsley	65 mL
¼ cup	chopped fresh chives	65 mL
4 oz.	cream cheese	120 g
¼ tsp.	ground black pepper	1 mL

- In a medium glass bowl, mix the grated zucchini, vinegar, sugar, and salt. Allow to sit at room temperature for 1 hour.
- Finely chop the parsley and chives.
- In a small bowl, soften the cream cheese.
- Strain the marinated zucchini through a single layer of cheesecloth, squeezing out as much of the liquid as possible.
- Place the strained zucchini in a food processor with a blade attachment. Add the softened cream cheese, parsley, chives, and black pepper. Process until a smooth paste forms.
- Transfer the finished mix into a small glass bowl. Cover and refrigerate.

Chef's notes: Use this paté as a spread for cold sandwiches in place of butter or margarine or as a topping on baked potatoes. • Pipe paté onto small toast rounds or crackers for canapés.

About the Author

Master Chef John Butler is an educator, food stylist, and author. He has won many awards and honours over his career, and in 2001 he was the first Canadian to win the Julia Child Scholarship, which was matched by support from the International Association of Culinary Professionals Foundation. John contributed recipes to Lois Hole's best-selling book *Herbs and Edible Flowers*, and his collection *A Treasury of Cookbook Classics* has sold more than one million copies worldwide. John lives in St. Albert and teaches at the Northern Alberta Institute of Technology in Edmonton.

Credits

Zucchini cartoon, page 16,
courtesy of Lynne Fahnestalk; used with permission.

Chocolate Zucchini Cake recipe, page 14,
from *Winners: More Recipes from The Best of Bridge* (1988).
Courtesy of Best of Bridge Publishing, Calgary, Alberta;
used with permission.

Cover art and interior illustrations by Donna McKinnon.

Book design by Gregory Brown.

Horticultural information prepared by Jim Hole and Earl J. Woods.